ELEMENTARY LIBRARY LESSON PLANS

+ LIBRARY CARD TEMPLATES

A FULL-YEAR CURRICULUM AND STUDENT WORKSHEETS FOR K-6TH GRADE STUDENTS

Name: *Lillie Monroe*

Grade: K 1st 2nd 3rd 4th 5th 6th

☐ ☐ ■ ☐ ☐ ☐ ☐

Reading Goal: *90%*

BARCODE

K

1.0	1.1	1.2	1.3	1.4	1.5	1.6	1.7	1.8	1.9
2.0	2.1	2.2	2.3	2.4	2.5	2.6	2.7	2.8	2.9
3.0	3.1	3.2	3.3	3.4	3.5	3.6	3.7	3.8	3.9

KG

4.0	4.1	4.2	4.3	4.4	4.5	4.6	4.7	4.8	4.9
5.0	5.1	5.2	5.3	5.4	5.5	5.6	5.7	5.8	5.9
6.0	6.1	6.2	6.3	6.4	6.5	6.6	6.7	6.8	6.9

7.0+

by Keshia L. Gaines, Ph.D.

Elementary Library Lesson Plans

A Full-Year Curriculum and Student Worksheets for K-6th Grade Students

Keshia L. Gaines, Ph.D.

iUniverse®

ELEMENTARY LIBRARY LESSON PLANS
A FULL-YEAR CURRICULUM AND STUDENT WORKSHEETS
FOR K-6TH GRADE STUDENTS

iUniverse books may be ordered through booksellers or by contacting:

iUniverse
1663 Liberty Drive
Bloomington, IN 47403
www.iuniverse.com
1-800-Authors (1-800-288-4677)

ISBN: 978-1-5320-5666-6 (sc)
ISBN: 978-1-5320-5667-3 (e)

Print information available on the last page.

iUniverse rev. date: 02/18/2019

TABLE OF CONTENTS

(3.) Lesson Plans and Worksheets for the 3rd Nine Weeks

(4.) Lesson Plans and Worksheets for the 4th Nine Weeks

Introduction

Elementary Librarians,

This lesson plan book is designed to save you time. Instead of spending hundreds of hours crafting lesson plans and worksheets, you can customize the included lesson plans and student worksheets in minutes. Just photocopy and you are done!

There are three keys to library class success:

- ✓ Awesome Lesson Plans
- ✓ Awesome Student Worksheets
- ✓ Awesome Library Cards

Awesome Lesson Plans

Dr. Keshia L. Gaines has provided everything that elementary librarians need to ensure that students are knowledgeable about library topics and are able to use an entire range of print and electronic resources. These lesson plans and student worksheets are designed to meet national standards and AASL® Standards. More importantly, Dr. Gaines creates simple universal lesson plans, which enable librarians to use variations of the same library topic and lesson plan to teach students from kindergarten through 6th grade. By merely adjusting the complexity of the lesson, students of different age levels can be engaged and learning necessary skills. Most elementary librarians teach multiple grade levels. Now, librarians only need one lesson plan to modify for each grade level. Universal lesson plans save time and make sense.

Awesome Student Worksheets

The included student worksheets were designed to address many national standards while maintaining the flexibility to customize them with state standards. The child-friendly designs make learning about library resources exciting. These worksheets can be used as a library class supplement or as a weekly homework assignment. You will find drawing activities, puzzles, vocabulary exercises, book reports, and more. All student worksheets include vocabulary words and a fun lesson or writing activity.

Awesome Library Card

The secret to success is the elementary library card! This new library card was designed by Dr. Gaines to help elementary students easily find resources on their correct reading level. After students are tested, their reading levels can be color-coded onto the library card to match the color-coded reading levels of the books in your library. With this new library card, students will easily learn their reading level and be able to identify books and resources accordingly. Dr. Gaines has designed many different versions of the universal library card for elementary students. The most popular version of the card features one simple boxed area for kindergarten students and one simple boxed area for students who read above a 7th grade level. Book check out is so much easier because students have a color-coded graphic to help them find books on their correct reading level (see Appendix C and Appendix D).

QUICK TIP- Collaborate with the art teacher(s) and others in the art department for help with adding barcodes and student reading levels to library cards. Students can work on this task as a part of an art class assignment. This will save you a lot of time and also serve as a collaborative lesson plan opportunity.

Elementary Library Lesson Plans offers resources not included in other library lesson plan books such as:

- ✓ weekly universal lesson plans
- ✓ child-friendly student worksheets
- ✓ easy-to-use library card templates
- ✓ circulation desk poster pad format
- ✓ yearly curriculum map

How to Use This Book

Although these lesson plans require minimal additional planning, there are a few things that you can add to these ready-made lessons to make your library class more successful. Before you use the lesson plan of the week and it's matching worksheet, you will see that you can alter certain parts of the lesson to make it more compatible with your library class. You can choose to create presentation slides to outline the lesson or give individual student notebooks to accompany the worksheets for additional writing space.

NOTE: The supplemental worksheets were designed for students in 3rd through 6th grades, but may be used with children as young as kindergarten. For younger students, the worksheet's directions may have to be read to them and answered verbally. When the vocabulary words are too advanced for a particular group of students, you can either have students find the beginning letters and sounds in the word or put the words in ABC order.

How do I Teach the Same Vocabulary Words to Every Grade Level?

Even a veteran librarian might wonder how to accomplish teaching one set of vocabulary words to students ranging from kindergarten to 6th grade. With these universal lesson plans, you can adjust the way that the vocabulary words are taught. Here are some suggestions that might work with your library classes.

Kindergarten	Have students find the vocabulary words by looking for the beginning letter. Focus on phonics and letter recognition. Students can find smaller words inside the larger ones.
1st grade	Have students practice reading the vocabulary words with fluency and accuracy. Explain the definition to them verbally.
2nd grade	Have students use the vocabulary words while discussing story elements and key details.
3rd grade	Have students apply the vocabulary words while practicing comprehension activities.
4th grade	Have students integrate knowledge and ideas across various types of literature.
5th grade	Have students analyze the vocabulary word's definition.
6th grade	Have students integrate knowledge and ideas to create sentences with the vocabulary words.

NOTE: The vocabulary words at the bottom of each worksheet page can help students in various ways. One suggestion is to allow students to write the definition of each word from a dictionary, cut the words into small cards to play a game, or practice spelling and sentence writing.

Since you know your students best, feel free to incorporate these lessons as you see fit. To save time and paper, you might consider making double sided copies of the worksheets. This will mean only one trip to the copy machine every two weeks. Students can complete one side per week and review the previous lesson too. Another idea is to make one-sided copies of the worksheets and allow the back side to be additional space for completing a journal activity, defining this week's vocabulary words, or writing a reflection of the lesson.

These lesson plans and student worksheets are designed to complement a 30-45 minute weekly library class. In general, the lessons progress in difficulty level and build on previously learned information. When you introduce the first lesson and worksheet, you might want to complete the lesson as a class until the students are comfortable with the routine and can work independently.

For special needs students or students who have language barriers, preview each lesson and make any adjustments ahead of time. Some students may need to do an alternative lesson, work as a small group, skip sections, or complete the lesson as a class. Although the worksheets vary in difficulty and time needed, once students are familiar with the routine, many will be able to complete the worksheet in 10 to 15 minutes.

A Look Inside

Each lesson plan includes the following features.

- ✓ **Lesson Number and Letter-** helps you easily organize lessons
- ✓ **Grade Level, Subject, and Fill-in Teacher/Librarian Space**
- ✓ **Title of the Lesson**- each title matches its corresponding worksheet
- ✓ **Objective-** this week's objective written from the librarian's perspective
- ✓ **"I can" statement-** this week's objective written from the student's perspective
- ✓ **Library Standards-** AASL standards condensed for time and space
- ✓ **Current State Standards-** add specific Common Core State Standards or other state standards that apply to this lesson
- ✓ **Materials Needed-** a helpful suggestion list of what you will need before you teach the lesson
- ✓ **Book of the Week-** a space for you to add at least one book title of your choice that complements that week's lesson
- ✓ **Procedures-** step-by-step instructions of suggested steps to take while teaching the lesson plans
- ✓ **Assignment-** includes completing the worksheet and learning the vocabulary words for the week
- ✓ **Assessment-** gives a brief formative assessment for each week's lesson
- ✓ **Additional Information Statement-** general statement and specific strategy for helping students with special needs, language barriers, or early lesson finishers

About the Author

Keshia L. Gaines, Ph.D.

Keshia L. Gaines, Ph.D. is an internationally recognized author, educator, and inventor in the areas of education and non-traditional learning methods. Dr. Gaines has been active in public education for over 15 years. As a young educator, Gaines works hard to create innovative methods for increasing student achievement. Dr. Gaines is the founder of Bus-stop 2 Bus-stop, LLC, a company that specializes in educational books, products, clothing, and services.

The academic background of Dr. Gaines includes a Bachelors of Arts (B.A.) in English from The University of Southern Mississippi, a Masters in Education (M.Ed.) from William Carey College, and a Doctorate of Philosophy (Ph.D.) in Educational Leadership from The University of Southern Mississippi.

Dr. Gaines has worked with elementary, middle school, and high school students in several school districts. Her experience includes teaching both general education and exceptional education students. Currently, she holds a MS educator license with endorsements in Art, Elementary Education, English, Exceptional Education, Library Media Specialist, and School Administration.

Send your library success stories and photos to Dr. Gaines's Mailbox! Write keshgaines@yahoo.com or visit www.facebook.com/drgainesmagazine for the latest news and updates.

Week 1A

Grade Level: K-6th **Subject: Library Skills** **Teacher/Librarian:**

MONDAY- FRIDAY **Title: "Welcome to the Library (Library Rules and Expectations)"**	
Objective **"I can" statement**	Students will be able to follow all library rules. I can follow all library rules.
Library Standards **Current State Standards**	1.2.2 making independent resource choices 3.1.6 using information and technology responsibly Grade Level: K 1st 2nd 3rd 4th 5th 6th Strand Taught: [ ] ______
Materials Needed	1. Worksheet 1A; 2. notebook paper and notecards; 3. short video on library rules (optional); 4. library rules; 5. Book of the Week:
Procedures	1. Students will go to the appropriate seating area. 2. The librarian will welcome students to the library and teach the library rules. 3. The librarian will read an excerpt from the book of the week. 4. Students will verbally answer comprehension questions about the book. 5. Students will use Worksheet 1A to write the library rules. 6. If time permits, students will review vocabulary words on notecards. 7. Students will tour the library and learn proper book check out procedures.
Assignment	Complete Worksheet 1A and learn this week's vocabulary words. **Vocabulary Words** barcode, character, monitor rules, patron, expectations wander, spine, inquire
Assessment	Formative Assessment: Quick Summary Race 1. Students will verbally summarize the library rules in 10-15 words. 2. As a group, students will explain the library rules to their peers.
Additional Information	**Accommodations and Modifications** The librarian will assist students as needed. Students in need of extra help will receive interventions consisting of varied instructional strategies. **Strategy of the Week:** Provide additional graphic organizers and writing space for library rules. **Early Finishers** Students will practice the academic vocabulary words listed above.

Worksheet 1A

"Welcome to the Library (Library Rules and Expectations)"

DIRECTIONS:

Write five library rules that you learned today.

1.

2.

3.

4.

5.

Vocabulary

barcode	character	monitor
rules	patron	expectations
wander	spine	inquire

Grade Level: K-6th   Subject: Library Skills   Teacher/Librarian:

MONDAY- FRIDAY Title: "Book Care Basics and Library Rules Review"	
Objective **"I can" statement**	Students will be able to properly take care of library books. I can take care of my library book(s).
LIBRARY Standards **Current State Standards**	3.3.1 respect other's diverse perspectives 2.3.1 make real world connections Grade Level: K 1st 2nd 3rd 4th 5th 6th Strand Taught: [ ] _____ _____
Materials Needed	1. Worksheet 1B 4. book care rules 2. construction paper and popsicle sticks 5. Book of the Week: 3. damaged books
Procedures	1. Students will go to the appropriate seating area. 2. The librarian will briefly review the library rules and introduce today's lesson. 3. The librarian will read an excerpt from the book of the week. 4. Students will verbally answer comprehension questions about the book. 5. Students will examine several damaged books and learn about book care. 6. If time permits, students will study this week's vocabulary words. 7. Students will review book care strategies and library rules again before class ends.
Assignment	Complete Worksheet 1B and learn this week's vocabulary words. **Vocabulary Words** <table><tr><td>borrow</td><td>examine</td><td>abbreviate</td></tr><tr><td>avoid</td><td>vindicate</td><td>harsh</td></tr><tr><td>solicit</td><td>frail</td><td>prosperity</td></tr></table>

Assessment	Formative Assessment: Popsicle Stick Pick
	   1. Students will verbally answer five questions (about book care) on a popsicle stick.
	   2. As a group, students will discuss several book care strategies.

Additional Information	**Accommodations and Modifications** The librarian will assist students as needed. Students in need of extra help will receive interventions consisting of varied instructional strategies. **Strategy of the Week:** Provide several opportunities for the student(s) to restate the information. **Early Finishers** Students will practice the academic vocabulary words listed above.

Worksheet 1B

"Book Care Basics and Library Rules Review"

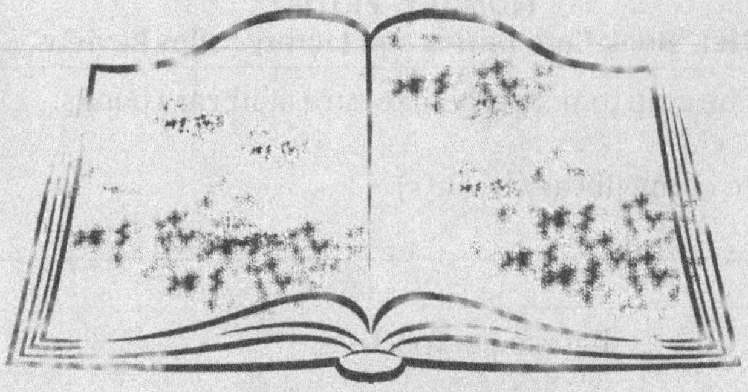

DIRECTIONS:

Write about two book care strategies.

1.

2.

Vocabulary

borrow	examine	abbreviate
avoid	vindicate	harsh
solicit	frail	prosperity

Grade Level: K-6th   **Subject:** Library Skills   **Teacher/Librarian:**

<table>
<tr>
<td colspan="2" align="center">MONDAY- FRIDAY
Title: "Shelf Markers, Book Ends, and Library Cards"</td>
</tr>
<tr>
<td>Objective

"I can" statement</td>
<td>Students will be able to utilize library helpers such as shelf markers, book ends, and library cards to help them in the library.

I can use library helpers such as shelf markers, book ends, and library cards to help me in the library.</td>
</tr>
<tr>
<td>LIBRARY Standards

Current State Standards</td>
<td>2.2.1   seeking additional helpful resources

4.4.6   select engaging and appropriate resources

Grade Level: K   1st   2nd   3rd   4th   5th   6th
Strand Taught: [   ] _____
_____</td>
</tr>
<tr>
<td>Materials Needed</td>
<td>

1. Worksheet 1C	4. dictionaries
2. file folders	5. Book of the Week:
3. stopwatch or timer	

</td>
</tr>
<tr>
<td>Procedures</td>
<td>1. Students will go to the appropriate seating area.
2. The librarian will briefly review last week's lesson and introduce today's lesson.
3. The librarian will read an excerpt from the book of the week.
4. Students will verbally answer questions about the book.
5. Students will use Worksheet 1C to learn about this week's objective.
6. If time permits, students will review vocabulary words.
7. Students will start checking out books this week.</td>
</tr>
<tr>
<td>Assignment</td>
<td>Complete Worksheet 1C and review vocabulary words.

Vocabulary Words

loan	compassion	temporary
method	placement	determine
pause	scrutinize	sequence

</td>
</tr>
<tr>
<td>Assessment</td>
<td>Formative Assessment: File Folders Game
   1. As a group, students will work together and write facts (from today's lesson) inside a file folder. The group that writes the most facts in five minutes is the winner.</td>
</tr>
<tr>
<td>Additional Information</td>
<td align="center">Accommodations and Modifications
The librarian will assist students as needed. Students in need of extra help will receive interventions consisting of varied instructional strategies.
Strategy of the Week:
Provide concrete examples of shelf markers, book ends, and library cards as a visual aid.
Early Finishers
Students will practice the academic vocabulary words listed above.</td>
</tr>
</table>

Worksheet 1C

"Shelf Markers, Book Ends, and Library Cards"

DIRECTIONS:

Help Dr. Gaines find the library card.

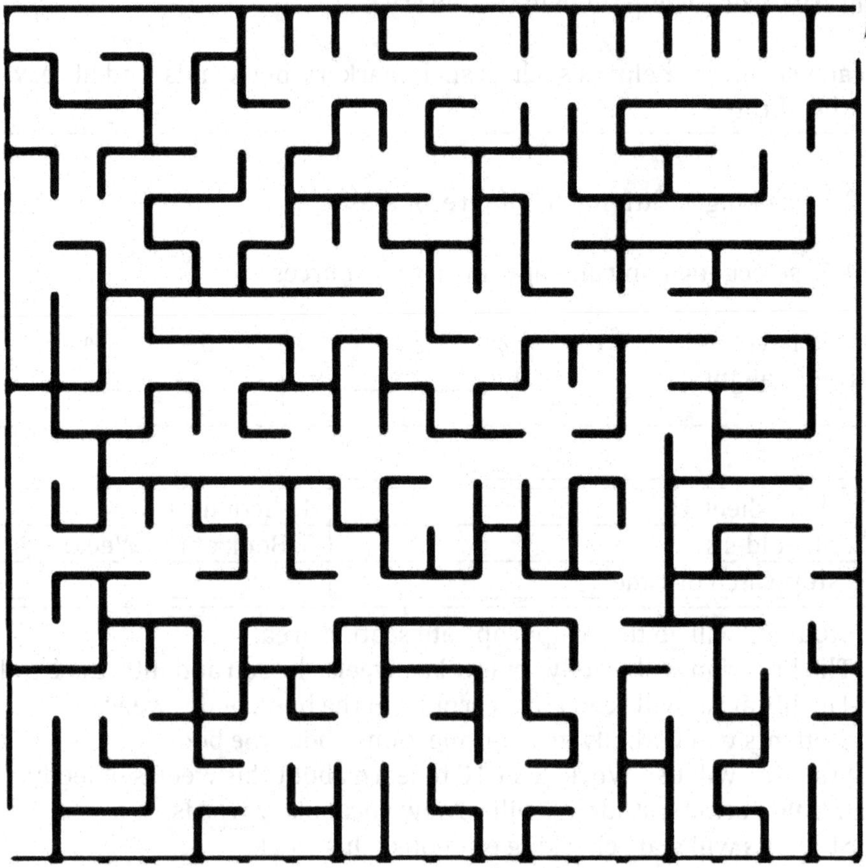

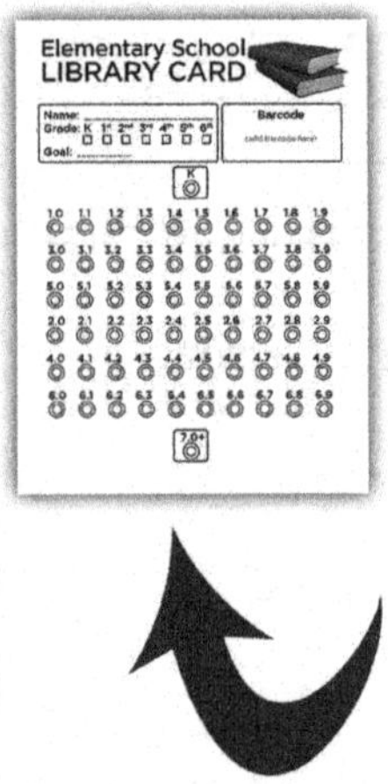

Write about two things you learned today.

____

____

Vocabulary

loan	compassion	temporary
method	placement	determine
pause	scrutinize	sequence

Grade Level: K-6th   **Subject:** Library Skills   **Teacher/Librarian:**

<table>
<tr><td colspan="2" align="center">MONDAY- FRIDAY
Title: "Fiction vs. Non-fiction"</td></tr>
<tr>
<td>Objective

"I can" statement</td>
<td>Students will be able to identify fiction and non-fiction books.

I can tell the difference between a fiction book and a non-fiction book.</td>
</tr>
<tr>
<td>LIBRARY Standards

Current State Standards</td>
<td>4.3.2 create resources for a purpose

3.1.5 connect learning to community issues

Grade Level: K   1st   2nd   3rd   4th   5th   6th
Strand Taught: [   ] _____
_____</td>
</tr>
<tr>
<td>Materials Needed</td>
<td>
<table>
<tr><td>1. Worksheet 1D</td><td>4. short video: fiction vs. non-fiction</td></tr>
<tr><td>2. drawing paper</td><td>5. Book of the Week:</td></tr>
<tr><td>3. fiction and non-fiction animal books</td><td></td></tr>
</table>
</td>
</tr>
<tr>
<td>Procedures</td>
<td>1. Students will go to the appropriate seating area.
2. The librarian will briefly review last week's lesson and introduce today's lesson.
3. The librarian will read an excerpt from the book of the week.
4. Students will verbally answer questions about the book.
5. Students will use Worksheet 1D to learn about this week's objective.
6. If time permits, students will define the vocabulary words.
7. Students will check in their library books and check out different ones.</td>
</tr>
<tr>
<td>Assignment</td>
<td>Complete Worksheet 1D and review vocabulary words.

Vocabulary Words
<table>
<tr><td>resources</td><td>advantage</td><td>gradual</td></tr>
<tr><td>fine</td><td>discredit</td><td>circulation</td></tr>
<tr><td>fiction</td><td>procrastinate</td><td>connect</td></tr>
</table>
</td>
</tr>
<tr>
<td>Assessment</td>
<td>Formative Assessment: Sketch-it-out
1. Students will draw one animal from a fiction book and one animal from a non-fiction book. As a group, students will discuss the differences between the books.</td>
</tr>
<tr>
<td>Additional Information</td>
<td align="center">Accommodations and Modifications
The librarian will assist students as needed. Students in need of extra help will receive interventions consisting of varied instructional strategies.
Strategy of the Week:
Provide a display (visual aid) of several fiction books and several non-fiction books.
Early Finishers
Students will practice the academic vocabulary words listed above.</td>
</tr>
</table>

Worksheet 1D

"Fiction vs. Non-fiction"

DIRECTIONS:

Compare and contrast a fiction book and a non-fiction book about dogs.

Fiction	Non-fiction

Vocabulary

resources	advantage	gradual
fine	discredit	circulation
fiction	procrastinate	connect

Week 1E

Grade Level: K-6th **Subject: Library Skills** **Teacher/Librarian:**

MONDAY- FRIDAY **Title: "Library Catalog Searches"**	
Objective **"I can" statement**	Students will be able to independently perform library catalog searches. I can search for a book or library resource using the library catalog.
LIBRARY Standards **Current State Standards**	4.4.1 identify areas of self-interest 1.2.6 persistence in information searches Grade Level: K 1st 2nd 3rd 4th 5th 6th Strand Taught: [ ] ______
Materials Needed	1. Worksheet 1E; 4. dictionaries 2. construction paper; 5. Book of the Week: 3. pretend TV show props
Procedures	1. Students will go to the appropriate seating area. 2. The librarian will briefly review last week's lesson and introduce today's lesson. 3. The librarian will read an excerpt from the book of the week. 4. Students will verbally answer questions about the book. 5. Students will use Worksheet 1E to learn about this week's objective. 6. If time permits, students will review academic vocabulary. 7. Students will check in their library books and check out different ones.
Assignment	Complete Worksheet 1E and the formative assessment. Vocabulary Words catalog, congregation, enable bookmark, renewal, arrange author, software, diagram
Assessment	Formative Assessment: Pretend TV Show 1. In a television show format, students will explain three facts from today's lesson. 2. As a group, students will explain the steps to complete a library catalog search.
Additional Information	**Accommodations and Modifications** The librarian will assist students as needed. Students in need of extra help will receive interventions consisting of varied instructional strategies. **Strategy of the Week:** Provide additional time and peer helpers during library catalog searches. **Early Finishers** Students will practice the academic vocabulary words listed above.

Worksheet 1E

"Library Catalog Searches"

DIRECTIONS:

Write several examples of each.

Book Titles	Book Authors	Book Subjects

Vocabulary

catalog	congregation	enable
bookmark	renewal	arrange
author	software	diagram

Week 1F

Grade Level: K-6th **Subject:** Library Skills **Teacher/Librarian:**

<table>
<tr><th colspan="2">MONDAY- FRIDAY
Title: "Internet Resources and Computer Skills- Part 1"</th></tr>
<tr><td>Objective

"I can" statement</td><td>Students will be able to use the Internet and computer resources properly.

I can use the Internet and computer resources properly.</td></tr>
<tr><td>LIBRARY Standards

Current State Standards</td><td>2.4.1 Accept, reject, or modify information

4.3.4 Practice ethical behaviors with electronics

Grade Level: K 1st 2nd 3rd 4th 5th 6th
Strand Taught: [ ] ________________________________
________________________________</td></tr>
<tr><td>Materials Needed</td><td><table><tr><td>1. Worksheet 1F</td><td>4. desktop or laptop computers</td></tr><tr><td>2. red and green construction paper</td><td>5. Book of the Week:</td></tr><tr><td>3. short video on computers (optional)</td><td></td></tr></table></td></tr>
<tr><td>Procedures</td><td>1. Students will go to the appropriate seating area.
2. The librarian will briefly review last week's lesson and introduce today's lesson.
3. The librarian will read an excerpt from the book of the week.
4. Students will verbally answer questions about the book.
5. Students will use Worksheet 1F to learn vocabulary relating to this week's objective.
6. If time permits, students will practice additional vocabulary words.
7. Students will check in their library books and check out different ones.</td></tr>
<tr><td>Assignment</td><td>Complete Worksheet 1F and review vocabulary words.

Vocabulary Words<table><tr><td>accept</td><td>hypothesis</td><td>electronic</td></tr><tr><td>reject</td><td>recall</td><td>interaction</td></tr><tr><td>modify</td><td>incompatible</td><td>compromise</td></tr></table></td></tr>
<tr><td>Assessment</td><td>Formative Assessment: Green YES, Red NO
1. The librarian will ask students five questions about the Internet and computers. Students will show green (yes) and/or red (no) cards to answer the questions.</td></tr>
<tr><td>Additional Information</td><td>Accommodations and Modifications
The librarian will assist students as needed. Students in need of extra help will receive interventions consisting of varied instructional strategies.
Strategy of the Week:
Provide a checklist of Internet and computer tasks for students to practice.
Early Finishers
Students will practice the academic vocabulary words listed above.</td></tr>
</table>

Worksheet 1F

"Internet Resources and Computer Skills - Part 1"

DIRECTIONS:

Find the words hidden in the puzzle below.

Computer Words Wordsearch

z	b	w	q	f	a	w	u	d	w	m	z	l	k	n
j	x	y	m	u	f	i	s	c	r	e	e	n	u	a
c	m	u	p	o	i	p	o	t	y	i	s	u	v	c
x	c	z	l	o	q	t	t	q	f	y	k	w	m	t
g	c	o	s	a	i	f	s	l	x	i	h	i	m	b
q	e	m	m	h	p	n	x	z	j	c	l	d	o	d
w	m	v	l	p	u	t	t	x	s	l	k	e	n	b
e	h	q	s	b	u	t	o	e	e	o	e	a	i	m
m	d	l	q	a	v	t	d	p	r	s	y	x	t	i
x	o	i	i	k	v	c	e	o	x	e	b	l	o	p
e	k	p	t	d	s	e	x	r	w	p	o	d	r	w
k	t	p	e	m	m	d	i	f	d	n	a	v	t	z
w	i	y	g	n	x	n	k	k	h	f	r	l	u	e
d	r	m	b	c	u	r	s	o	r	z	d	l	h	f
m	o	u	s	e	d	t	m	h	z	b	n	p	b	h

mouse
pointer
file
open
keyboard
quit
screen
close
edit
laptop
shutdown
save
cursor
monitor
computer

Vocabulary

accept	hypothesis	electronic
reject	recall	interaction
modify	incompatible	compromise

Week 1G

Grade Level: K-6th **Subject:** Library Skills **Teacher/Librarian:**

MONDAY- FRIDAY **Title: "Story Elements in Fiction Books"**	
Objective **"I can" statement**	Students will be able to identify all story elements in a fiction book. I can identify the characters, setting, plot, conflict, and resolution within a story.
LIBRARY Standards **Current State Standards**	4.1.2 Make connections with the reading. 2.1.3 Apply knowledge to real world situations. Grade Level: K 1st 2nd 3rd 4th 5th 6th Strand Taught: [ ] ______________
Materials Needed	1. Worksheet 1G; 4. video on story elements (optional) 2. white paper for postcards; 5. Book of the Week: 3. example book: *Little Red Riding Hood*
Procedures	1. Students will go to the appropriate seating area. 2. The librarian will briefly review last week's lesson and introduce today's lesson. 3. The librarian will read an excerpt from the book of the week. 4. Students will verbally answer questions about the book excerpt. 5. Students will use Worksheet 1G to learn about this week's objective. 6. If time permits, students will research the story elements on the Internet. 7. Students will check in their library books and check out different ones.
Assignment	Complete Worksheet 1G and review vocabulary words. Vocabulary Words hold, collaborate, opponent elements, fortunate, journey origin, reclusive, mystify
Assessment	Formative Assessment: Parent Postcards 1. Students will summarize today's lesson by creating a postcard to their parent(s). 2. As a group, students will discuss today's lesson.
Additional Information	**Accommodations and Modifications** The librarian will assist students as needed. Students in need of extra help will receive interventions consisting of varied instructional strategies. **Strategy of the Week:** Provide the story of *Little Red Riding Hood* as an audio book or as a video story. **Early Finishers** Students will practice the academic vocabulary words listed above.

Worksheet 1G

"Story Elements in Fiction Books"

DIRECTIONS:

Write the story elements for *Little Red Riding Hood.*

characters | setting | plot | conflict | resolution

Vocabulary

hold	collaborate	opponent
elements	fortunate	journey
origin	reclusive	mystify

Week 1H

Grade Level: K-6th **Subject: Library Skills** **Teacher/Librarian:**

MONDAY- FRIDAY **Title: "The Dewey Decimal Classification System- Part 1"**	
Objective **"I can" statement**	Students will be able to find library books using the Dewey Decimal Classification System. I can find books using the Dewey Decimal Classification System.
LIBRARY Standards **Current State Standards**	3.2.3 Work with others as a team. 1.2.3 Use multiple resources and formats. Grade Level: K 1st 2nd 3rd 4th 5th 6th Strand Taught: [ ] ____________
Materials Needed	1. Worksheet 1H; 2. pencils or pens; 3. Dewey Decimal System Chart; 4. notebook paper (optional); 5. Book of the Week:
Procedures	1. Students will go to the appropriate seating area. 2. The librarian will briefly review last week's lesson and introduce today's lesson. 3. The librarian will read an excerpt from the book of the week. 4. Students will verbally answer questions about the book of the week. 5. Students will use Worksheet 1H to learn about this week's objective. 6. If time permits, students will review last week's lesson. 7. Students will check in their library books and check out different ones.
Assignment	Complete Worksheet 1H and review vocabulary words. **Vocabulary Words** average, teamwork, classification DVD, serials, arid habit, format, productive
Assessment	Formative Assessment: Journal Topic (Write about opening your own restaurant.) Describe the restaurant, the employees, and the foods served there. 1. As a group, students will discuss their journal topic responses. 2. BONUS QUESTION: What library resource could you use to find out more information about opening your own restaurant?
Additional Information	**Accommodations and Modifications** The librarian will assist students as needed. Students in need of extra help will receive interventions consisting of varied instructional strategies. **Strategy of the Week:** Provide mnemonics for students to remember the Dewey Decimal System. **Early Finishers** Students will practice the academic vocabulary words listed above.

Worksheet 1H

"The Dewey Decimal Classification System- Part 1"

DIRECTIONS:

Create a name for your own restaurant.

____

Using the Dewey Decimal Classification System,
explain where books about cooking can be found in a library.

____

Describe your restaurant, the employees, and the foods served there.

____

____

____

Draw a picture of your restaurant here.

Vocabulary

average	teamwork	classification
DVD	serials	arid
habit	format	productive

Week 1I

Grade Level: K-6th **Subject: Library Skills** **Teacher/Librarian:**

MONDAY- FRIDAY **Title: "Reference Books"**	
Objective **"I can" statement**	Students will be able to identify reference books and describe their purposes. I can use an atlas, encyclopedia, dictionary, thesaurus and other reference books properly.
LIBRARY Standards **Current State Standards**	4.1.4 Seek information for personal learning. 1.4.4 Seek help appropriately. Grade Level: K 1st 2nd 3rd 4th 5th 6th Strand Taught: [ ] ______________________ ______________________
Materials Needed	1. Worksheet 1I; 4. video on reference books (optional) 2. notebook paper; 5. Book of the Week: 3. different types of reference books
Procedures	1. Students will go to the appropriate seating area. 2. The librarian will briefly review last week's lesson and introduce today's lesson. 3. The librarian will read an excerpt from the book of the week. 4. Students will verbally answer questions about the book. 5. Students will use Worksheet 1I to learn about this week's objective. 6. If time permits, students will practice the vocabulary words. 7. Students will check in their library books and check out different ones.
Assignment	Complete Worksheet 1I and review vocabulary words. Vocabulary Words atlas, thesaurus, appropriate dictionary, encyclopedia, extension reference, seek, advice
Assessment	Formative Assessment: Exit Ticket 1. Students will list five types of reference books. 2. As a group, students will practice defining vocabulary words as a game.
Additional Information	**Accommodations and Modifications** The librarian will assist students as needed. Students in need of extra help will receive interventions consisting of varied instructional strategies. **Strategy of the Week:** Provide reference books in large print and electronic reference resources. **Early Finishers** Students will practice the vocabulary words listed above.

Worksheet 1I

"Reference Books"

atlas | encyclopedia | dictionary | thesaurus | almanac

DIRECTIONS:

Write several reasons why reference books are helpful.

Vocabulary

atlas	thesaurus	appropriate
dictionary	encyclopedia	extension
reference	seek	advice

Grade Level: K-6th   Subject: Library Skills   Teacher/Librarian:

	MONDAY- FRIDAY **Title: "Intellectual Property"**
Objective **"I can" statement**	Students will be able to recognize publication dates and copyright symbols. I can recognize the publication date and a copyright symbol in a book.
LIBRARY Standards **Current State Standards**	1.3.1 Respect copyrighted intellectual property. 3.3.7 Respect intellectual freedom. Grade Level: K 1st 2nd 3rd 4th 5th 6th Strand Taught: [ ] _____ _____
Materials Needed	<table><tr><td>1. Worksheet 2A</td><td>4. dictionaries</td></tr><tr><td>2. large trademark and copyright symbols</td><td>5. Book of the Week:</td></tr><tr><td>3. shelf markers</td><td></td></tr></table>
Procedures	1. Students will go to the appropriate seating area. 2. The librarian will briefly review last week's lesson and introduce today's lesson. 3. The librarian will read an excerpt from the book of the week. 4. Students will verbally answer questions about the book. 5. Students will use Worksheet 2A to learn about this week's objective. 6. If time permits, students will practice defining vocabulary words. 7. Students will check in their library books and check out different ones.
Assignment	Complete Worksheet 2A and review the vocabulary words. Vocabulary Words <table><tr><td>property</td><td>intellectual</td><td>chronological</td></tr><tr><td>copyright</td><td>publication</td><td>bibliography</td></tr><tr><td>respect</td><td>creator</td><td>symbol</td></tr></table>
Assessment	Formative Assessment: Find Three Copyright Dates 1. As a group, students will find the copyright dates of three randomly selected books.
Additional Information	**Accommodations and Modifications** The librarian will assist students as needed. Students in need of extra help will receive interventions consisting of varied instructional strategies. **Strategy of the Week:** Provide graphic organizers to help students learn about intellectual property. **Early Finishers** Students will practice the vocabulary words listed above.

Worksheet 2A

"Intellectual Property"

DIRECTIONS:

Draw a picture of a copyright symbol here.

Find the words hidden in the puzzle.

C	U	L	K	K	H	T	Y	J	B	C	I	B	P	K
K	H	S	S	P	Q	T	X	P	A	N	R	I	N	F
I	H	R	S	Y	R	Z	M	Z	T	O	O	B	V	N
W	T	T	O	E	M	V	D	E	M	X	T	L	T	M
N	W	H	P	N	Y	B	L	A	X	X	A	I	J	L
Y	R	O	G	J	O	L	O	V	W	M	E	O	L	N
H	R	E	X	I	E	L	H	L	T	H	R	G	T	J
P	B	B	S	C	R	X	O	Z	H	K	C	R	B	D
G	L	I	T	P	P	Y	N	G	C	C	E	A	I	G
F	K	U	X	S	E	J	P	J	I	Z	Y	P	S	Q
N	A	M	T	T	V	C	D	O	N	C	R	H	R	Z
L	X	S	Y	A	K	Q	T	J	C	T	A	Y	W	V
P	U	B	L	I	C	A	T	I	O	N	K	L	B	T
Z	T	Q	L	A	R	F	Y	X	U	K	U	I	F	Q
A	X	P	H	W	H	X	E	C	E	Y	I	B	M	P

BIBLIOGRAPHY
CHRONOLOGICAL
COPYRIGHT
CREATOR
INTELLECTUAL
PROPERTY
PUBLICATION
RESPECT
SYMBOL

What is intellectual property?

Vocabulary

property	intellectual	chronological
copyright	publication	bibliography
respect	creator	symbol

Grade Level: K-6th   Subject: Library Skills   Teacher/Librarian:

<table>
<tr><td colspan="2" align="center">MONDAY- FRIDAY
Title: "Using Maps and Globes- Part 1"</td></tr>
<tr>
<td>Objective

"I can" statement</td>
<td>Students will be able to use a map and a globe to locate specific areas.

I can use a map and a globe to locate specific areas.</td>
</tr>
<tr>
<td>LIBRARY Standards

Current State Standards</td>
<td>3.1.4 Use information tools wisely.

4.3.1 Social exchange of ideas.

Grade Level: K   1st   2nd   3rd   4th   5th   6th
Strand Taught: [   ] _____

_____</td>
</tr>
<tr>
<td>Materials Needed</td>
<td>
<table>
<tr><td>1. Worksheet 2B</td><td>4. large atlas</td></tr>
<tr><td>2. class sets of maps</td><td>5. Book of the Week:</td></tr>
<tr><td>3. globe</td><td></td></tr>
</table>
</td>
</tr>
<tr>
<td>Procedures</td>
<td>1. Students will go to the appropriate seating area.
2. The librarian will briefly review last week's lesson and introduce today's lesson.
3. The librarian will read an excerpt from the book of the week.
4. Students will verbally answer questions about the book.
5. Students will use Worksheet 2B to learn about this week's objective.
6. If time permits, students will review the vocabulary words.
7. Students will check in their library books and check out different ones.</td>
</tr>
<tr>
<td>Assignment</td>
<td>Complete Worksheet 2B and review the vocabulary words.

Vocabulary Words
<table>
<tr><td>map</td><td>predict</td><td>ordeal</td></tr>
<tr><td>organize</td><td>opulent</td><td>periodical</td></tr>
<tr><td>globe</td><td>distant</td><td>atlas</td></tr>
</table>
</td>
</tr>
<tr>
<td>Assessment</td>
<td>Formative Assessment: Sketch a Map of Your School Library
    1. Students will sketch a map of their school library and label each section.
    2. As a group, students will answer basic questions about today's book of the week.</td>
</tr>
<tr>
<td>Additional Information</td>
<td align="center">Accommodations and Modifications
The librarian will assist students as needed. Students in need of extra help will receive interventions consisting of varied instructional strategies.
Strategy of the Week:
Provide graph paper for students that need more structure to create a map.
Early Finishers
Students will practice the vocabulary words listed above.</td>
</tr>
</table>

Worksheet 2B

"Using Maps, Globes, and Atlases- Part 1"

DIRECTIONS:

Draw a map of your school's library. Label the fiction, non-fiction, and other areas of the library.

MY SCHOOL LIBRARY MAP

Vocabulary

map	predict	ordeal
organize	opulent	periodical
globe	distant	atlas

Week 2C

Grade Level: K-6th **Subject: Library Skills** **Teacher/Librarian:**

<table>
<tr><td colspan="2">MONDAY- FRIDAY
Title: "All About Magazines"</td></tr>
<tr><td>Objective

"I can" statement</td><td>Students will be able to recognize a magazine and the contents inside a magazine.

I can recognize a magazine and its parts.</td></tr>
<tr><td>LIBRARY Standards

Current State Standards</td><td>4.2.3 Seek information about new ideas.

1.2.1 Posing questions and investigating answers

Grade Level: K 1st 2nd 3rd 4th 5th 6th
Strand Taught: [ ] ______________________
______________________</td></tr>
<tr><td>Materials Needed</td><td>
<table>
<tr><td>1. Worksheet 2C</td><td>4. five different children's magazines</td></tr>
<tr><td>2. large chart paper</td><td>5. Magazine of the Week:</td></tr>
<tr><td>3. magazine advertisements</td><td></td></tr>
</table>
</td></tr>
<tr><td>Procedures</td><td>1. Students will go to the appropriate seating area.
2. The librarian will briefly review last week's lesson and introduce today's lesson.
3. The librarian will read a magazine article from a children's magazine.
4. Students will verbally answer questions about the magazine article.
5. Students will use Worksheet 2C to learn about this week's objective.
6. If time permits, students will discuss 1 magazine articles about animals.
7. Students will check in their library books and check out different ones.</td></tr>
<tr><td>Assignment</td><td>Complete Worksheet 2C and review the vocabulary words.

Vocabulary Words
<table>
<tr><td>magazine</td><td>abundant</td><td>headline</td></tr>
<tr><td>newspaper</td><td>reference</td><td>illustrator</td></tr>
<tr><td>section</td><td>comparison</td><td>category</td></tr>
</table>
</td></tr>
<tr><td>Assessment</td><td>Formative Assessment: Compare and Contrast- Magazines vs. Books
1. Students will compare and contrast magazines and books using a chart.
2. As a group, students will complete an exit slip about today's lesson.</td></tr>
<tr><td>Additional Information</td><td>Accommodations and Modifications
The librarian will assist students as needed. Students in need of extra help will receive interventions consisting of varied instructional strategies.
Strategy of the Week:
Provide physical copies and electronic versions of child-friendly magazines.
Early Finishers
Students will practice the academic vocabulary words listed above.</td></tr>
</table>

Worksheet 2C

"All About Magazines"

DIRECTIONS:

Compare and contrast magazines and books.

Write the characteristics of each in the boxes below.

MAGAZINES	BOOKS

Vocabulary

magazine	abundant	headline
newspaper	reference	illustrator
section	comparison	category

Week 2D

Grade Level: K-6th **Subject: Library Skills** **Teacher/Librarian:**

<table>
<tr><td colspan="2">MONDAY- FRIDAY
Title: "Story Predictions"</td></tr>
<tr><td>Objective

"I can" statement</td><td>Students will be able to predict the plot of a book by analyzing the title and book cover.

I can predict the plot of a book by looking at the title and book cover.</td></tr>
<tr><td>LIBRARY Standards

Current State Standards</td><td>4.1.6 Organize personal knowledge easily.

1.3.2 Seek divergent information perspectives.

Grade Level: K 1st 2nd 3rd 4th 5th 6th
Strand Taught: [ ] ____________________
____________________</td></tr>
<tr><td>Materials Needed</td><td>1. Worksheet 2D | 4. dictionaries
2. five fiction books | 5. Book of the Week:
3. shelf markers |</td></tr>
<tr><td>Procedures</td><td>1. Students will go to the appropriate seating area.
2. The librarian will briefly review last week's lesson and introduce today's lesson.
3. The librarian will read an excerpt from the book of the week.
4. Students will verbally answer questions about the book.
5. Students will use Worksheet 2D to learn about this week's objective.
6. If time permits, students will review vocabulary words.
7. Students will check in their library books and check out different ones.</td></tr>
<tr><td>Assignment</td><td>Complete Worksheet 2D and review the vocabulary words.

Vocabulary Words
index | dominant | distinction
account | prediction | opponent
refrain | phase | appropriate</td></tr>
<tr><td>Assessment</td><td>Formative Assessment: Predict that Story Game
1. Students will be assessed by verbally answering questions about today's book.
2. As a group, students will race to predict the plots of five different fiction books.</td></tr>
<tr><td>Additional Information</td><td>Accommodations and Modifications
The librarian will assist students as needed. Students in need of extra help will receive interventions consisting of varied instructional strategies.
Strategy of the Week:
Provide preferential seating to students in need of extra help.
Early Finishers
Students will practice the academic vocabulary words listed above.</td></tr>
</table>

Worksheet 2D

"Story Predictions"

DIRECTIONS:

Look at the cover of one fiction book in your library.

Write 3-5 sentences about your story prediction based off of the book's cover.

Vocabulary

index	dominant	distinction
account	prediction	opponent
refrain	phase	appropriate

Week 2E

<table>
<tr><th colspan="2">MONDAY- FRIDAY
Title: "Understanding Mystery Books"</th></tr>
<tr><td>Objective

"I can" statement</td><td>Students will be able to identify and understand mystery books.

I can identify and understand mystery books.</td></tr>
<tr><td>LIBRARY Standards

Current State Standards</td><td>2.4.2 Reflect on process and assess investigation.
2.2.2 Formulate and test alternative conclusions
2.2.3 Evidence leads to a conclusion or decision

Grade Level: K 1st 2nd 3rd 4th 5th 6th
Strand Taught: [ ] ____________________
____________________</td></tr>
<tr><td>Materials Needed</td><td><table><tr><td>1. Worksheet 2E</td><td>4. index cards</td></tr><tr><td>2. construction paper</td><td>5. Book of the Week:</td></tr><tr><td>3. mystery books</td><td></td></tr></table></td></tr>
<tr><td>Procedures</td><td>1. Students will go to the appropriate seating area.
2. The librarian will briefly review last week's lesson and introduce today's lesson.
3. The librarian will read an excerpt from the book of the week.
4. Students will verbally answer questions about the book.
5. Students will use Worksheet 2E to learn about this week's objective.
6. If time permits, students will practice vocabulary words.
7. Students will check in their library books and check out different ones.</td></tr>
<tr><td>Assignment</td><td>Complete Worksheet 2E and review the vocabulary words.

Vocabulary Words<table><tr><td>achieve</td><td>dominant</td><td>interpretation</td></tr><tr><td>mystery</td><td>reserve</td><td>criticize</td></tr><tr><td>narrative</td><td>liability</td><td>apparatus</td></tr></table></td></tr>
<tr><td>Assessment</td><td>Formative Assessment: Mystery Match- Index Card Sort
1. Students will be assessed by verbally answering questions about mystery books.
2. As a group, students will sort index cards with this week's vocabulary words.</td></tr>
<tr><td>Additional Information</td><td>Accommodations and Modifications
The librarian will assist students as needed. Students in need of extra help will receive interventions consisting of varied instructional strategies.
Strategy of the Week:
Provide study sheets and teacher outlines of the lesson.
Early Finishers
Students will practice the academic vocabulary words listed above.</td></tr>
</table>

Worksheet 2E

"Understanding Mystery Books"

DIRECTIONS:

Help the students find their favorite mystery books.

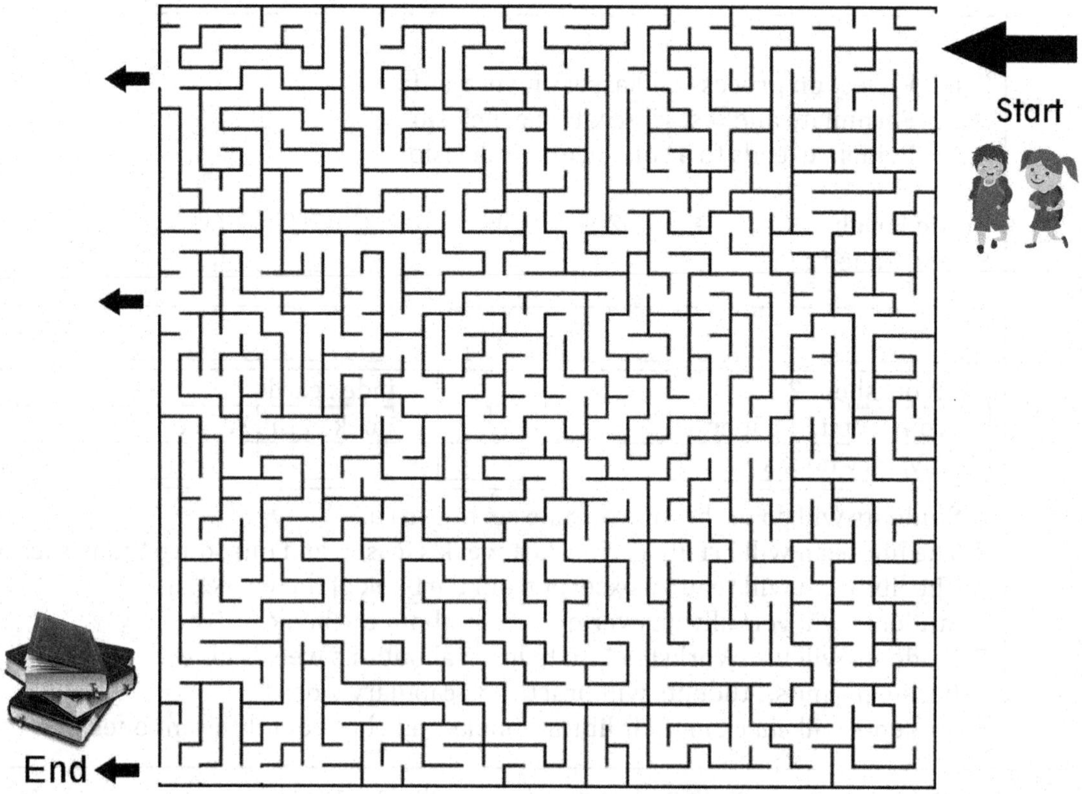

Write the titles of three mystery books.

1. ______________________
2. ______________________
3. ______________________

Vocabulary

achieve	dominant	interpretation
mystery	reserve	criticize
narrative	liability	apparatus

Week 2F

Grade Level: K-6th **Subject: Library Skills** **Teacher/Librarian:**

<table>
<tr><td colspan="2">MONDAY- FRIDAY
Title: "Internet Resources and Computer Skills- Part 2"</td></tr>
<tr><td>Objective

"I can" statement</td><td>Students will be able to proficiently use Internet resources and computer programs.

I can use the Internet and the computer programs.</td></tr>
<tr><td>LIBRARY Standards

Current State Standards</td><td>1.1.8 Demonstrate mastery of technology tools.

2.1.4 Use technology to analyze and organize.

Grade Level: K 1st 2nd 3rd 4th 5th 6th
Strand Taught: [ ] ____________________
____________________</td></tr>
<tr><td>Materials Needed</td><td><table><tr><td>1. Worksheet 2F</td><td>4. dictionaries</td></tr><tr><td>2. large keyboard poster</td><td>5. Book of the Week:</td></tr><tr><td>3. computer with Internet</td><td></td></tr></table></td></tr>
<tr><td>Procedures</td><td>1. Students will go to the appropriate seating area.
2. The librarian will briefly review last week's lesson and introduce today's lesson.
3. The librarian will read an excerpt from the book of the week.
4. Students will verbally answer questions about the book.
5. Students will use Worksheet 2F to learn about this week's objective.
6. If time permits, students will practice vocabulary words.
7. Students will check in their library books and check out different ones.</td></tr>
<tr><td>Assignment</td><td>Complete Worksheet 2F and review the vocabulary words.

Vocabulary Words<table><tr><td>keyboard</td><td>sufficient</td><td>pamphlet</td></tr><tr><td>Internet</td><td>adversity</td><td>access</td></tr><tr><td>priority</td><td>denied</td><td>competition</td></tr></table></td></tr>
<tr><td>Assessment</td><td>Formative Assessment: Four Area Discussion- Synonym, Antonym, Picture, Sentence
1. Students will be assessed by verbally discussing the definition of "Internet."
2. As a group, students will discuss the four areas for the word "computer."</td></tr>
<tr><td>Additional Information</td><td>Accommodations and Modifications
The librarian will assist students as needed. Students in need of extra help will receive interventions consisting of varied instructional strategies.
Strategy of the Week:
Provide extra visual and verbal cues and prompts.
Early Finishers
Students will practice the academic vocabulary words listed above.</td></tr>
</table>

Worksheet 2F

"Internet Resources and Computer Skills - Part 2"

DIRECTIONS:

Evaluate a children's website.

1. Write the name of the children's website here.

2. Does this website have helpful information?

3. What type of information can be learned from this website?

4. Do all of the links work?

5. Who is the author of this website?

6. Does this website have advertisements?

7. Do you like this website?

Vocabulary

keyboard	sufficient	pamphlet
Internet	adversity	access
priority	denied	competition

Week 2G

Grade Level: K-6th **Subject: Library Skills** **Teacher/Librarian:**

MONDAY- FRIDAY **Title: "The Table of Contents and the Index"**	
Objective **"I can" statement**	Students will be able to identify and use the table of contents and index to find information in a book. I can use a table of contents and an index properly.
LIBRARY Standards **Current State Standards**	2.1.2 Organize and use knowledge. 1.1.7 Make sense of information gathered. Grade Level: K 1st 2nd 3rd 4th 5th 6th Strand Taught: [ ] ____________________ ____________________
Materials Needed	1. Worksheet 2G; 4. example index 2. construction paper for mini books; 5. Book of the Week: (non-fiction title) 3. example table of contents
Procedures	1. Students will go to the appropriate seating area. 2. The librarian will briefly review last week's lesson and introduce today's lesson. 3. The librarian will read an excerpt from the book of the week. 4. Students will verbally answer questions about the book. 5. Students will use Worksheet 2G to learn about this week's objective. 6. If time permits, students will practice this week's vocabulary words. 7. Students will check in their library books and check out different ones.
Assignment	Complete Worksheet 2G and review the vocabulary words. Vocabulary Words glossary, prove, irrelevant category, aesthetic, stacks index, enhance, occupy
Assessment	Formative Assessment: Literary Mini-Books- Table of Contents and Index 1. Students will create non-fiction mini-books with a table of contents and an index. 2. As a group, students will complete an exit slip summary about today's lesson.
Additional Information	**Accommodations and Modifications** The librarian will assist students as needed. Students in need of extra help will receive interventions consisting of varied instructional strategies. **Strategy of the Week:** Provide verbal and visual cues regarding directions and staying on task. **Early Finishers** Students will practice the academic vocabulary words listed above.

Worksheet 2G

"The Table of Contents and the Index"

DIRECTIONS:

Create a table of contents for a short non-fiction book about cars.

Write the definition of <u>index</u>.

Vocabulary

glossary	prove	irrelevant
category	aesthetic	stacks
index	enhance	occupy

Grade Level: K-6th   **Subject:** Library Skills   **Teacher/Librarian:**

	MONDAY- FRIDAY **Title: "Poetry- Create Your Own Poem"**
Objective "I can" statement	Students will be able to identify and create poems. I know what a poem is and I can create a poem.
LIBRARY **Standards** **Current State** **Standards**	2.1.1 Apply critical thinking skills (analysis, synthesis, evaluation, organization.) 3.4.2 Review and assess the quality of the learning product. Grade Level: K 1ˢᵗ 2ⁿᵈ 3ʳᵈ 4ᵗʰ 5ᵗʰ 6ᵗʰ Strand Taught: [ ] _____ _____
Materials **Needed**	1. Worksheet 2H 4. instrumental music 2. construction paper 5. Book of the Week: (poetry book) 3. individual poems
Procedures	1. Students will go to the appropriate seating area. 2. The librarian will briefly review last week's lesson and introduce today's lesson. 3. The librarian will read an excerpt from the book of the week. 4. Students will verbally answer questions about the book. 5. Students will use Worksheet 2H to learn about this week's objective. 6. If time permits, students will review vocabulary words. 7. Students will check in their library books and check out different ones.
Assignment	Complete Worksheet 2H and review the vocabulary words. Vocabulary Words <table><tr><td>poem</td><td>simile</td><td>stanza</td></tr><tr><td>entertain</td><td>headings</td><td>congregation</td></tr><tr><td>rhyme</td><td>amicable</td><td>omit</td></tr></table>
Assessment	Formative Assessment: Rhyming Poem Project 1. As a group, students will write a rhyming poem to upbeat instrumental music.
Additional **Information**	**Accommodations and Modifications** The librarian will assist students as needed. Students in need of extra help will receive interventions consisting of varied instructional strategies. **Strategy of the Week:** Provide audio or video recorders for students to record their poems. **Early Finishers** Students will practice the academic vocabulary words listed above.

Worksheet 2H

"Poetry- Create Your Own Poem"

DIRECTIONS:

Use some of the words listed below to create your own poem about a book.

words	poem
cover spine title page publisher copyright date author illustrator illustrations barcode call number	

Vocabulary

poem	simile	stanza
entertain	headings	congregation
rhyme	amicable	omit

Week 2I

Grade Level: K-6th **Subject:** Library Skills **Teacher/Librarian:**

MONDAY- FRIDAY Title: "Mini-Book Report 1"	
Objective **"I can" statement**	Students will be able to complete mini-book report 1 using the provided template. I can complete mini-book report 1.
LIBRARY Standards **Current State Standards**	3.1.2 Participate as a network of learners. 1.4.2 Use feedback from teachers and peers. Grade Level: K 1st 2nd 3rd 4th 5th 6th Strand Taught: [ ] ________________
Materials Needed	1. Worksheet 2I; 2. construction paper for exit slips; 3. notebook paper; 4. dictionaries; 5. Book of the Week:
Procedures	1. Students will go to the appropriate seating area. 2. The librarian will briefly review last week's lesson and introduce today's lesson. 3. The librarian will read an excerpt from the book of the week. 4. Students will verbally answer questions about the book. 5. Students will use Worksheet 2I to learn about this week's objective. 6. If time permits, students will practice vocabulary words. 7. Students will check in their library books and check out different ones.
Assignment	Complete Worksheet 2I and review the vocabulary words. Vocabulary Words annual, curriculum, misspelled report, anachronistic, interruption indent, trace, analysis
Assessment	Formative Assessment: Book Report Review 1. Students will be assessed by verbally answering questions about the book. 2. As a group, students will complete an exit slip about today's lesson.
Additional Information	**Accommodations and Modifications** The librarian will assist students as needed. Students in need of extra help will receive interventions consisting of varied instructional strategies. **Strategy of the Week:** Provide positive feedback and no penalty for spelling errors or sloppy handwriting. **Early Finishers** Students will practice the academic vocabulary words listed above.

Worksheet 2I

"Mini-Book Report 1"

DIRECTIONS:

Create a fiction book report.

Book Title: ______________________ Author: __________________ No. of Pages: ______

Publisher : ____________________________________ Copyright Date: ____________

Where and when did the to story take place?

List the main characters:

Write a brief summary of the book (beginning, middle, and end).

Write two new words that you learned from the book and then write the definition of these words.

1.

2.

Evaluate the book : 1 2 3 4 5 6 7 8 9 10

Vocabulary

annual	curriculum	misspelled
report	anachronistic	interruption
indent	trace	analysis

Grade Level: K-6th   **Subject:** Library Skills   **Teacher/Librarian:**

	MONDAY- FRIDAY **Title: "Library Vocabulary Camp"**
Objective **"I can" statement**	Students will be able to explain vocabulary definitions. I can learn vocabulary definitions.
LIBRARY Standards **Current State Standards**	1.1.6 Make inferences and gather meaning. 3.4.1 Investigate the learning process. Grade Level: K 1st 2nd 3rd 4th 5th 6th Strand Taught: [ ] _____ _____
Materials Needed	<table><tr><td>1. Worksheet 3A</td><td>4. dictionaries</td></tr><tr><td>2. notebook paper</td><td>5. Book of the Week:</td></tr><tr><td>3. peer evaluation form</td><td></td></tr></table>
Procedures	1. Students will go to the appropriate seating area. 2. The librarian will briefly review last week's lesson and introduce today's lesson. 3. The librarian will read an excerpt from the book of the week. 4. Students will verbally answer questions about the book. 5. Students will use Worksheet 3A to learn about this week's objective. 6. If time permits, students will practice vocabulary words. 7. Students will check in their library books and check out different ones.
Assignment	Complete Worksheet 3A and review the vocabulary words. Vocabulary Words <table><tr><td>opinion</td><td>anecdote</td><td>essential</td></tr><tr><td>benefit</td><td>database</td><td>questionnaire</td></tr><tr><td>adverb</td><td>merit</td><td>irritation</td></tr></table>

Assessment	Formative Assessment: Peer Evaluation Form
	    1. Students will be assessed by verbally answering questions about the book.
	    2. As a group, students will write three vocabulary words with its definition.

Additional Information	**Accommodations and Modifications** The librarian will assist students as needed. Students in need of extra help will receive interventions consisting of varied instructional strategies. **Strategy of the Week:** Provide use of computers and electronic devices for finding definitions. **Early Finishers** Students will practice the academic vocabulary words listed above.

Worksheet 3A

"Library Vocabulary Camp"

DIRECTIONS:

Write the definition of the word blurb. Create a short blurb for a new fiction book about children in an elementary school.

What is a blurb?	Create a short blurb.

Vocabulary

opinion	anecdote	essential
benefit	database	questionnaire
adverb	merit	irritation

Week 3B

Grade Level: K-6th   Subject: Library Skills   Teacher/Librarian:

MONDAY- FRIDAY Title: "Dewey Decimal Classification System: Part 2"	
Objective **"I can" statement**	Students will be able to effectively use the Dewey Decimal Classification System to find non-fiction books in the library. I can use the Dewey Decimal Classification System to find books in the library.
LIBRARY Standards **Current State Standards**	4.4.2 Recognize personal knowledge. 1.4.1 Adapt/monitor processes for effectiveness. Grade Level: K 1st 2nd 3rd 4th 5th 6th Strand Taught: [ ] ____________________ ____________________
Materials Needed	1. Worksheet 3B / 4. dictionaries 2. fact sheet about Melvil Dewey / 5. Book of the Week: 3. vocabulary word cards
Procedures	1. Students will go to the appropriate seating area. 2. The librarian will briefly review last week's lesson and introduce today's lesson. 3. The librarian will read an excerpt from the book of the week. 4. Students will verbally answer questions about the book. 5. Students will use Worksheet 3B to learn about this week's objective. 6. If time permits, students will practice vocabulary words. 7. Students will check in their library books and check out different ones.
Assignment	Complete Worksheet 3B and review the vocabulary words. Vocabulary Words strategy / bibliography / poetry media / collage / anonymous author / dedication / username
Assessment	Formative Assessment: Pros & Cons Exit Slip 1. Students will be assessed by verbally answering questions about Melvil Dewey. 2. As a group, students will shelve two fiction books and two non-fiction books.
Additional Information	**Accommodations and Modifications** The librarian will assist students as needed. Students in need of extra help will receive interventions consisting of varied instructional strategies. **Strategy of the Week:** Provide visual and verbal cues and prompts for learning the Dewey Decimal System. **Early Finishers** Students will practice the academic vocabulary words listed above.

Worksheet 3B

"Dewey Decimal Classification System - Part 2"

DIRECTIONS:

Create a dewey decimal system poster that explains how a dewey decimal system works.

Dewey Decimal System Poster

Vocabulary

strategy	bibliography	poetry
media	collage	anonymous
author	dedication	username

Week 3C

Grade Level: K-6th **Subject:** Library Skills **Teacher/Librarian:**

<table>
<tr><td colspan="2">MONDAY- FRIDAY
Title: "Fairy Tales & Folk Tales"</td></tr>
<tr><td>Objective

"I can" statement</td><td>Students will be able to identify and understand fairy tales and folk tales.

I can understand fairy tales and folk tales.</td></tr>
<tr><td>LIBRARY Standards

Current State Standards</td><td>1.2.4 Question the validity and accuracy of information.

4.2.4 Expressing interest in various literary genres.

Grade Level: K 1st 2nd 3rd 4th 5th 6th
Strand Taught: [ ] ____________________
____________________</td></tr>
<tr><td>Materials Needed</td><td>1. Worksheet 3C | 4. dictionaries
2. fairy tales and folk tales | 5. Book of the Week:
3. video story of a fairy tale (optional)</td></tr>
<tr><td>Procedures</td><td>1. Students will go to the appropriate seating area.
2. The librarian will briefly review last week's lesson and introduce today's lesson.
3. The librarian will read an excerpt from the book of the week.
4. Students will verbally answer questions about the book.
5. Students will use Worksheet 3C to learn about this week's objective.
6. If time permits, students will practice vocabulary words.
7. Students will check in their library books and check out different ones.</td></tr>
<tr><td>Assignment</td><td>Complete Worksheet 3C and review the vocabulary words.

Vocabulary Words
whisper | genre | theme
bound | antagonist | illustration
source | fable | tale</td></tr>
<tr><td>Assessment</td><td>Formative assessment: Student Conference (1-on-1 or group)
1. Students will pretend to have a conference and discuss the differences between a fairy tale and a folk tale. Students will list several examples of fairy tales.</td></tr>
<tr><td>Additional Information</td><td>Accommodations and Modifications
The librarian will assist students as needed. Students in need of extra help will receive interventions consisting of varied instructional strategies.
Strategy of the Week:
Provide several examples of fairy tales and folk tales from the library.
Early Finishers
Students will practice the academic vocabulary words listed above.</td></tr>
</table>

Worksheet 3C

"Fairy Tales & Folk Tales"

DIRECTIONS:

Draw the fairy tale character using the grid.

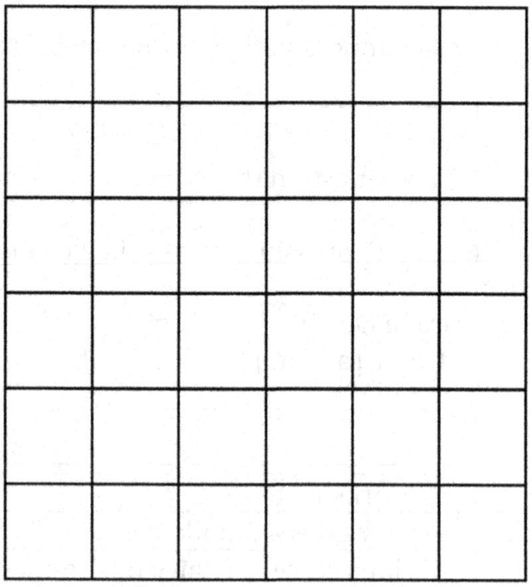

Write the titles of two fairy tales.

____

____

Vocabulary

whisper	genre	theme
bound	antagonist	illustration
source	fable	tale

Grade Level: K-6th   Subject: Library Skills   Teacher/Librarian:

MONDAY- FRIDAY Title: "All About Biographies"	
Objective "I can" statement	Students will be able to identify and understand biographies. I can identify and understand a biography.
LIBRARY Standards **Current State Standards**	3.3.6 Use information and knowledge. 1.2.5 Changing the inquiry focus, questions, resources, or strategies Grade Level: K 1st 2nd 3rd 4th 5th 6th Strand Taught: [ ] _____ _____
Materials Needed	1. Worksheet 3D 2. construction paper 3. pictures of famous people / 4. example biographies 5. Book of the Week: (a biography)
Procedures	1. Students will go to the appropriate seating area. 2. The librarian will briefly review last week's lesson and introduce today's lesson. 3. The librarian will read an excerpt from the book of the week. 4. Students will verbally answer questions about the book. 5. Students will use Worksheet 3D to learn about this week's objective. 6. If time permits, students will practice their vocabulary words 7. Students will check in their library books and check out different ones.
Assignment	Complete Worksheet 3D and review the vocabulary words.. Vocabulary Words <table><tr><td>realistic</td><td>occupation</td><td>autobiography</td></tr><tr><td>quote</td><td>collection</td><td>biography</td></tr><tr><td>setting</td><td>theme</td><td>misfortune</td></tr></table>
Assessment	Formative Assessment: Biography Bowl 1. Students will be assessed by answering questions about the book of the week. 2. As a group, students will answer three questions about biographies.
Additional Information	**Accommodations and Modifications** The librarian will assist students as needed. Students in need of extra help will receive interventions consisting of varied instructional strategies. **Strategy of the Week:** Provide computer links and additional resources for at home research of biographies. **Early Finishers** Students will practice the academic vocabulary words listed above.

Worksheet 3D

"All About Biographies"

DIRECTIONS:

Write about one famous person.

What is this person's birthdate? ______________________________

Where is he/she from? ______________________________

Name two positive things this famous person is known for.

1. ______________________________

2. ______________________________

Vocabulary

realistic	occupation	autobiography
quote	collection	biography
setting	theme	misfortune

Week 3E

Grade Level: K-6th **Subject: Library Skills** **Teacher/Librarian:**

MONDAY- FRIDAY Title: "Newspaper Articles and Parts of a Newspaper"	
Objective **"I can" statement**	Students will be able to identify the different parts of a newspaper. I can use a newspaper properly.
LIBRARY Standards **Current State Standards**	2.3.2 Diverse and global perspectives 3.3.5 Exchange ideas beyond the learning community. Grade Level: K 1st 2nd 3rd 4th 5th 6th Strand Taught: [ ] ________________
Materials Needed	1. Worksheet 3E; 2. construction paper for exit slips; 3. newspaper advertisements; 4. local newspaper copies; 5. Newspaper Article of the Week:
Procedures	1. Students will go to the appropriate seating area. 2. The librarian will briefly review last week's lesson and introduce today's lesson. 3. The librarian will read a short newspaper article to students. 4. Students will verbally answer questions about the newspaper article. 5. Students will use Worksheet 3E to learn about this week's objective. 6. If time permits, students will practice vocabulary words. 7. Students will check in their library books and check out different ones.
Assignment	Complete Worksheet 3E and review the vocabulary words. Vocabulary Words record, headline, periodical newspaper, assiduous, intelligent browse, comprehension, publisher
Assessment	Formative Assessment: Create a Newspaper Advertisement 1. Students will be assessed by verbally answering questions about the article. 2. As a group, students will create one newspaper advertisement.
Additional Information	**Accommodations and Modifications** The librarian will assist students as needed. Students in need of extra help will receive interventions consisting of varied instructional strategies. **Strategy of the Week:** Provide rest breaks and a quiet corner of the room for reading the newspaper. **Early Finishers** Students will practice the academic vocabulary words listed above.

"Newspaper Articles and Parts of a Newspaper"

DIRECTIONS:

Write a short newspaper article about the children in the picture.
Remember to create a headline.

CREATE A NEWSPAPER ARTICLE HERE

Vocabulary

record	headline	periodical
newspaper	assiduous	intelligent
browse	comprehension	publisher

Week 3F

Grade Level: K-6th **Subject: Library Skills** **Teacher/Librarian:**

MONDAY- FRIDAY **Title: "Exploring Graphic Novels and Comic Books"**	
Objective **"I can" statement**	Students will be able to identify and understand graphic novels and comic books. I can describe a graphic novel and a comic book.
LIBRARY Standards **Current State Standards**	4.1.1 Read and listen for pleasure. 3.2.1 Present ideas in formal and informal situations. Grade Level: K 1st 2nd 3rd 4th 5th 6th Strand Taught: [ ] ______
Materials Needed	1. Worksheet 3F; 2. drawing paper; 3. comic books; 4. graphic novels; 5. Comic Book of the Week:
Procedures	1. Students will go to the appropriate seating area. 2. The librarian will briefly review last week's lesson and introduce today's lesson. 3. The librarian will read an excerpt from a comic book to students. 4. Students will verbally answer questions about the comic book. 5. Students will use Worksheet 3F to learn about this week's objective. 6. If time permits, students will review vocabulary words. 7. Students will check in their library books and check out different ones.
Assignment	Complete Worksheet 3F and review the vocabulary words. Vocabulary Words: cartoon, imitate, panel; access, caption, protagonist; motion, sequential, digression
Assessment	Formative Assessment: Create a Comic Strip 1. Students will verbally answer questions about their comic strip. 2. As a group, students will complete an exit slip about today's lesson.
Additional Information	**Accommodations and Modifications** The librarian will assist students as needed. Students in need of extra help will receive interventions consisting of varied instructional strategies. **Strategy of the Week:** Provide adaptive writing utensils, paper, stencils and/or rulers to create comics. **Early Finishers** Students will practice the academic vocabulary words listed above.

Worksheet 3F

"Exploring Graphic Novels and Comic Books"

DIRECTIONS:

Create a comic strip by sketching illustrations and adding speech bubbles.

Vocabulary

cartoon	imitate	panel
access	caption	protagonist
motion	sequential	digression

Week 3G

Grade Level: K-6th **Subject: Library Skills** **Teacher/Librarian:**

MONDAY- FRIDAY **Title: "Dictionary vs. Thesaurus"**	
Objective **"I can" statement**	Students will be able to search for words in a dictionary and a thesaurus. I can use a dictionary and a thesaurus:
LIBRARY Standards **Current State Standards**	4.4.3 Focus efforts in personal learning 1.1.4 Find, evaluate, and select sources Grade Level: K 1st 2nd 3rd 4th 5th 6th Strand Taught: [ ] ______
Materials Needed	1. Worksheet 3G; 2. notebook paper; 3. children's dictionary; 4. children's thesaurus; 5. Dictionary Definitions of the Week:
Procedures	1. Students will go to the appropriate seating area. 2. The librarian will briefly review last week's lesson and introduce today's lesson. 3. The librarian will read 2 definitions to students from a children's dictionary. 4. Students will verbally answer questions about the dictionary. 5. Students will use Worksheet 3G to learn about this week's objective. 6. If time permits, students will practice this week's vocabulary words. 7. Students will check in their library books and check out different ones.
Assignment	Complete Worksheet 3G and review the vocabulary words. Vocabulary Words: criticize, orator, synonym required, label, glide dictionary, historical, thesaurus
Assessment	Formative Assessment: Question Blanks 1. Students will verbally answer questions about the dictionary and thesaurus. I am confused by ________. I understand ________.
Additional Information	**Accommodations and Modifications** The librarian will assist students as needed. Students in need of extra help will receive interventions consisting of varied instructional strategies. **Strategy of the Week:** Provide a children's dictionary and thesaurus with large print and color pictures. **Early Finishers** Students will practice the academic vocabulary words listed above.

Worksheet 3G

"Dictionary vs. Thesaurus"

DIRECTIONS:

Compare and contrast a dictionary and a thesaurus.

dictionary	thesaurus

Vocabulary

criticize	orator	synonym
required	label	glide
dictionary	historical	thesaurus

Grade Level: K-6th   Subject: Library Skills   Teacher/Librarian:

MONDAY- FRIDAY **Title: "Using Maps, Globes, and Atlases- Part 2"**	
Objective "I can" statement	Students will be able to properly use a map, globe, and atlas. I can use a map, globe, and atlas.
LIBRARY Standards **Current State Standards**	1.3.4 Exchange ideas within the learning community. 4.2.2 Trying a variety of formats Grade Level: K 1st 2nd 3rd 4th 5th 6th Strand Taught: [ ] _____ _____
Materials Needed	1. Worksheet 3H 4. globe 2. construction paper 5. Map of the Week: 3. United States map
Procedures	1. Students will go to the appropriate seating area. 2. The librarian will briefly review last week's lesson and introduce today's lesson. 3. The librarian will show example maps and atlases to students. 4. Students will verbally answer questions about the maps and/or atlases. 5. Students will use Worksheet 3H to learn about this week's objective. 6. If time permits, students will practice vocabulary words. 7. Students will check in their library books and check out different ones.
Assignment	Complete Worksheet 3H and review the vocabulary words. Vocabulary Words grasp — diagram — legend map — archives — camaraderie guide — historical — atlas
Assessment	Formative Assessment: Find that Location 1. Students will be assessed by their ability to find three different locations on a map. Also, students will find France, Russia, and China on a globe.
Additional Information	**Accommodations and Modifications** The librarian will assist students as needed. Students in need of extra help will receive interventions consisting of varied instructional strategies. **Strategy of the Week:** Provide a video or Internet link for additional information about maps. **Early Finishers** Students will practice the academic vocabulary words listed above.

© 2019 by Keshia L. Gaines, Ph.D.

Worksheet 3H

"Using Maps, Globes, and Atlases- Part 2"

DIRECTIONS:

Create a simple map of your city. Include your school and the area where you live.

Vocabulary

grasp	diagram	legend
map	archives	camaraderie
guide	historical	atlas

Week 3I

Grade Level: K-6th **Subject: Library Skills** **Teacher/Librarian:**

MONDAY- FRIDAY **Title: "Using an Encyclopedia"**	
Objective **"I can" statement**	Students will be able to use an encyclopedia (print and digital versions). I can use an encyclopedia (print and digital versions).
LIBRARY Standards **Current State Standards**	4.2.1 Pursue interests in multiple resources. 1.2.7 Pursue information for a broad perspective. Grade Level: K 1st 2nd 3rd 4th 5th 6th Strand Taught: [ ] ________________ ________________
Materials Needed	1. Worksheet 3I / 4. encyclopedia set 2. construction paper / 5. Encyclopedia Topic of the Week: 3. Internet encyclopedia (optional)
Procedures	1. Students will go to the appropriate seating area. 2. The librarian will briefly review last week's lesson and introduce today's lesson. 3. The librarian will read one page from a World Book® Encyclopedia. 4. Students will verbally answer questions about the encyclopedia. 5. Students will use Worksheet 3I to learn about this week's objective. 6. If time permits, students will write definitions for each vocabulary word. 7. Students will check in their library books and check out different ones.
Assignment	Complete Worksheet 3I and review the vocabulary words. Vocabulary Words intend / novice / reference encyclopedia / citation / index volume / launch / mythology
Assessment	Formative Assessment: 3-2-1, 3 ideas, 2 things learned, and 1 question 1. Students will be assessed by verbally answering questions about encyclopedias. 2. As a group, students will answer the 3-2-1 formative assessment.
Additional Information	**Accommodations and Modifications** The librarian will assist students as needed. Students in need of extra help will receive interventions consisting of varied instructional strategies. **Strategy of the Week:** Provide additional writing space for the lesson about encyclopedias. **Early Finishers** Students will practice the academic vocabulary words listed above.

Worksheet 3I

"Using an Encyclopedia"

DIRECTIONS:

Play 3-2-1 Encyclopedia Time.
Fill in the blanks as quickly as you can.

3 topics covered in an encyclopedia:

______________ ______________ ______________

2 things learned today:

______________ ______________

1 question I have about encyclopedias:

____

Vocabulary

intend	novice	reference
encyclopedia	citation	index
volume	launch	mythology

Grade Level: K-6th   Subject: Library Skills   Teacher/Librarian:

	MONDAY- FRIDAY **Title: "Library Safety and Rules Review"**		
Objective **"I can" statement**	Students will be able to remember all library rules and safety procedures. I can be safe and follow rules in the library.		
LIBRARY Standards **Current State Standards**	3.3.3 Engage in conversation around issues of concern. 4.4.4 Interpret based on cultural and social context. Grade Level: K 1st 2nd 3rd 4th 5th 6th Strand Taught: [ ] _____ _____		
Materials Needed	1. Worksheet 4A	4. library rules	
	2. toy microphone (pretend microphone)	5. Book of the Week:	
	3. pretend talk show props		
Procedures	1. Students will go to the appropriate seating area. 2. The librarian will briefly review last week's lesson and introduce today's lesson. 3. The librarian will read an excerpt from the book of the week. 4. Students will verbally answer questions about the book. 5. Students will use Worksheet 4A to learn about this week's objective. 6. If time permits, students will practice the vocabulary words of the week. 7. Students will check in their library books and check out different ones.		
Assignment	Complete Worksheet 4A and review the vocabulary words. Vocabulary Words		
	quiet	overdue	visualize
	individual	diligent	annotation
	librarian	paraphrase	spam
Assessment	Formative Assessment: Talk Show Time 1. In a talk show format, students will use the toy microphone to discuss library safety and library rules.		
Additional Information	**Accommodations and Modifications** The librarian will assist students as needed. Students in need of extra help will receive interventions consisting of varied instructional strategies. **Strategy of the Week:** Provide a study guide with at least five library rules. **Early Finishers** Students will practice the academic vocabulary words listed above.		

Worksheet 4A

"Library Safety and Rules Review"

DIRECTIONS:

Write about three library rules and how students can be safe in the library.

____

____

____

____

____

____

____

____

____

____

____

____

____

Vocabulary

quiet	overdue	visualize
individual	diligent	annotation
librarian	paraphrase	spam

Week 4B

Grade Level: K-6th **Subject: Library Skills** **Teacher/Librarian:**

MONDAY- FRIDAY Title: "Intellectual Property Review"	
Objective **"I can" statement**	Students will be able to understand copyright, intellectual property, and library ethics. I can understand copyright, intellectual property, and library ethics.
LIBRARY Standards **Current State Standards**	2.3.3 Use information to make ethical decisions. 1.3.3 Follow ethical and legal guidelines. Grade Level: K 1st 2nd 3rd 4th 5th 6th Strand Taught: [ ] ______
Materials Needed	1. Worksheet 4B; 4. copyright symbol example 2. construction paper; 5. Book of the Week: 3. trademark symbol example
Procedures	1. Students will go to the appropriate seating area. 2. The librarian will briefly review last week's lesson and introduce today's lesson. 3. The librarian will read an excerpt from the book of the week. 4. Students will verbally answer questions about the book. 5. Students will use Worksheet 4B to learn about this week's objective. 6. If time permits, students will practice vocabulary words. 7. Students will check in their library books and check out different ones.
Assignment	Complete Worksheet 4B and review the vocabulary words. Vocabulary Words cite, lobbyist, netiquette limit, copyright, frugal ethics, username, password
Assessment	Formative Assessment: Summary Poem 1. Students will compare and contrast a trademark symbol and a copyright symbol. 2. As a group, students will create a rhyming summary poem about today's lesson.
Additional Information	**Accommodations and Modifications** The librarian will assist students as needed. Students in need of extra help will receive interventions consisting of varied instructional strategies. **Strategy of the Week:** Provide an opportunity for the student(s) to answer the question verbally. **Early Finishers** Students will practice the academic vocabulary words listed above.

Worksheet 4B

"Intellectual Property Review"

copyrights | patents | trademarks

DIRECTIONS:

Draw and label a copyright symbol and a trademark symbol.

What is a patent?

Write the titles and copyright dates of three different books.

1.

2.

3.

Vocabulary

cite	lobbyist	netiquette
limit	copyright	frugal
ethics	username	password

Week 4C

Grade Level: K-6th **Subject: Library Skills** **Teacher/Librarian:**

MONDAY- FRIDAY Title: "Author Study- Dr. Theodore Seuss Geisel (Dr. Seuss)"	
Objective **"I can" statement**	Students will be able to recognize Dr. Seuss books and recall facts about him. I can recognize a Dr. Seuss book and tell facts about Dr. Seuss.
LIBRARY Standards **Current State Standards**	1.1.6 Read, view, and listen for information presented in any format (e.g., textual, visual, media, digital) in order to make inferences and gather meaning. 1.2.1 Display initiative and engagement by posing questions and investigating the answers beyond the collection of superficial facts. Grade Level: K 1st 2nd 3rd 4th 5th 6th Strand Taught: [ ] ________
Materials Needed	1. Worksheet 4C; 2. construction paper; 3. several Dr. Seuss books; 4. dictionaries; 5. Book of the Week: (a Dr. Seuss book)
Procedures	1. Students will go to the appropriate seating area. 2. The librarian will briefly review last week's lesson and introduce today's lesson. 3. The librarian will read an excerpt from the book of the week. 4. Students will verbally answer questions about the book. 5. Students will use Worksheet 4C to learn about this week's objective. 6. If time permits, students will practice vocabulary words. 7. Students will check in their library books and check out different ones.
Assignment	Complete Worksheet 4C and review the vocabulary words. Vocabulary Words observe, character, monitor volume, database, parched topic, spine, magnificent
Assessment	Formative Assessment: Quick Quiz 1. Students will verbally answer questions about Dr. Seuss and his books. 2. As a group, students will explain where Dr. Seuss books are found in the library.
Additional Information	**Accommodations and Modifications** The librarian will assist students as needed. Students in need of extra help will receive interventions consisting of varied instructional strategies. **Strategy of the Week:** Provide content from audiobooks, movies, videos, and digital media. **Early Finishers** Students will practice the academic vocabulary words listed above.

Worksheet 4C

"Author Study- Dr. Theodore Seuss Geisel (Dr. Seuss)"

Who is Dr. Seuss?

In what city, state, and year was Dr. Seuss born?

Why did Dr. Seuss write children's books?

Write the titles of three books created by Dr. Seuss.

1.

2.

3.

Vocabulary

observe	character	monitor
volume	database	parched
topic	spine	magnificent

Week 4D

Grade Level: K-6th **Subject: Library Skills** **Teacher/Librarian:**

MONDAY- FRIDAY **Title: "Create Your Own Mini-Book- Part 1 (Front Cover, Back Cover, and Spine)"**	
Objective **"I can" statement**	Students will be able to create a small fiction book with a front cover, back cover, spine, and interior pages. I can create a small fiction book with a front cover, back cover, spine, and interior pages.
LIBRARY Standards **Current State Standards**	4.3.3 Opportunities for personal and aesthetic growth. 2.1.6 Create products that express new understandings Grade Level: K 1st 2nd 3rd 4th 5th 6th Strand Taught: [ ] ______________________ ______________________
Materials Needed	1. Worksheet 4D; 2. construction paper; 3. drawing paper; 4. dictionaries; 5. Book of the Week:
Procedures	1. Students will go to the appropriate seating area. 2. The librarian will briefly review last week's lesson and introduce today's lesson. 3. The librarian will read an excerpt from the book of the week. 4. Students will verbally answer questions about the book. 5. Students will use Worksheet 4D to learn about this week's objective. 6. If time permits, students will practice vocabulary words. 7. Students will check in their library books and check out different ones.
Assignment	Complete Worksheet 4D and review the vocabulary words. Vocabulary Words mural, absorption, literature information, spine, integrity renew, paperback, chapter
Assessment	Formative Assessment: Movie Poster Drawing 1. Students will be assessed by verbally answering questions about today's lesson. 2. As a group, students will complete a pretend movie poster about today's book.
Additional Information	**Accommodations and Modifications** The librarian will assist students as needed. Students in need of extra help will receive interventions consisting of varied instructional strategies. **Strategy of the Week:** Provide a reduction in distractions as much as possible. **Early Finishers** Students will practice the academic vocabulary words listed above.

Worksheet 4D

"Create Your Own Mini-Book- Part 1 (Front Cover, Back Cover, and Spine)"

DIRECTIONS:

Create a draft of the front cover, back cover, and spine of your mini-book.

front cover	spine	back cover

Vocabulary

mural	absorption	literature
information	spine	integrity
renew	paperback	chapter

Week 4E

Grade Level: K-6th Subject: Library Skills Teacher/Librarian:

MONDAY- FRIDAY
Title: "Create Your Own Mini-Book- Part 2 (Interior Pages)"

Objective

"I can" statement

Students will be able to create a small fiction book with a front cover, back cover, spine, and interior pages.

I can create a small fiction book with a front cover, back cover, spine, and interior pages.

LIBRARY Standards

1.4.3 Monitor information for gaps or weaknesses.

4.4.5 Effectively gauge personal ideas

3.3.4 Create products for real-world contexts.

Current State Standards

Grade Level: K 1st 2nd 3rd 4th 5th 6th
Strand Taught: [ ] ______________________
____

Materials Needed

1. Worksheet 4E	4. dictionaries
2. sticky notes	5. Book of the Week:
3. blank sheets of paper	

Procedures

1. Students will go to the appropriate seating area.
2. The librarian will briefly review last week's lesson and introduce today's lesson.
3. The librarian will read an excerpt from the book of the week.
4. Students will verbally answer questions about the book.
5. Students will use Worksheet 4E to learn about this week's objective.
6. If time permits, students will practice vocabulary words.
7. Students will check in their library books and check out different ones.

Assignment

Complete Worksheet 4E and review the vocabulary words.

Vocabulary Words

character	emulate	genre
journal	nonchalant	exemplary
moisture	illustrator	series

Assessment

Formative Assessment: Sticky Notes

1. Each student will write this week's book summary on a sticky note.
2. If time permits, students will critique each other's mini-books.

Additional Information

Accommodations and Modifications

The librarian will assist students as needed. Students in need of extra help will receive interventions consisting of varied instructional strategies.

Strategy of the Week:

Provide additional graphic organizers and writing space.

Early Finishers

Students will practice the academic vocabulary words listed above.

Worksheet 4E

"Create Your Own Mini-Book- Part 2 (Interior Pages)"

DIRECTIONS:

Write several sentences about your mini-book's plot.

Vocabulary

character	emulate	genre
journal	nonchalant	exemplary
moisture	illustrator	series

Week 4F

Grade Level: K-6th **Subject: Library Skills** **Teacher/Librarian:**

MONDAY- FRIDAY **Title: "Book Fair vs. Reading Fair"**	
Objective **"I can" statement**	Students will be able to explain the purpose of a book fair and the procedure for purchasing books using money. Students will be able to complete a reading fair storyboard practice sheet for a fiction book. I can describe a book fair and use money to purchase books. I can complete a reading fair storyboard practice sheet for a fiction book
LIBRARY Standards **Current State Standards**	3.4.3 Work with others in a group setting. 2.1.5 Collaborate with others. Grade Level: K 1st 2nd 3rd 4th 5th 6th Strand Taught: [ ] ________________
Materials Needed	1. Worksheet 4F; 4. dictionaries 2. sentence strips; 5. Book of the Week: 3. book fair titles
Procedures	1. Students will go to the appropriate seating area. 2. The librarian will briefly review last week's lesson and introduce today's lesson. 3. The librarian will read an excerpt from the book of the week. 4. Students will verbally answer questions about the book and describe a book fair. 5. Students will use Worksheet 4F to learn about this week's objective. 6. If time permits, students will write out a book wish list. 7. Students will check in their library books and check out different ones.
Assignment	Complete Worksheet 4F and review the vocabulary words. Vocabulary Words money, technology, scanner keywords, exchange, barter receipt, tactful, outcome
Assessment	Formative Assessment: 1 Sentence Strip- Tell One Sentence 1. Students will verbally give a one-sentence summary of a book fair. 2. As a group, students will discuss their reading fair storyboard practice sheets.
Additional Information	**Accommodations and Modifications** The librarian will assist students as needed. Students in need of extra help will receive interventions consisting of varied instructional strategies. **Strategy of the Week:** Provide student-made examples to help students create reading fair storyboards. **Early Finishers** Students will practice the academic vocabulary words listed above.

Worksheet 4F

"Book Fair vs. Reading Fair"

DIRECTIONS:

In your own words, write a short definition for <u>book fair.</u>

DIRECTIONS:

On a separate sheet of paper, complete a reading fair practice sheet for a fiction book.

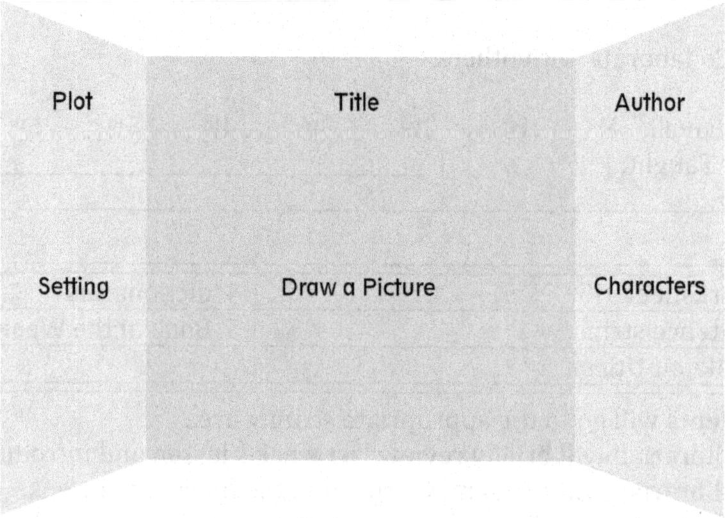

Vocabulary

money	technology	scanner
keywords	exchange	barter
receipt	tactful	outcome

Grade Level: K-6th   **Subject:** Library Skills   **Teacher/Librarian:**

MONDAY- FRIDAY	
Title: "Internet Resources and Computer Skills- Part 3 (Keyboard Practice)"	
Objective **"I can" statement**	Students will be able to use the Internet and computer programs properly. I can use the Internet and computer programs properly.
LIBRARY Standards **Current State Standards**	1.1.5 Evaluate for accuracy, validity, and appropriateness. 1.3.5 Use technology responsibly. Grade Level: K 1st 2nd 3rd 4th 5th 6th Strand Taught: [ ] _____ _____
Materials Needed	1. Worksheet 4G 4. dictionaries 2. drawing paper 5. Book of the Week: 3. 12" rulers
Procedures	1. Students will go to the appropriate seating area. 2. The librarian will briefly review last week's lesson and introduce today's lesson. 3. The librarian will read an excerpt from the book of the week. 4. Students will verbally answer questions about the book. 5. Students will use Worksheet 4G to learn about this week's objective. 6. If time permits, students will practice vocabulary words. 7. Students will check in their library books and check out different ones.
Assignment	Complete Worksheet 4G and review the vocabulary words. Vocabulary Words

remark	network	microfilm
primary	submissive	plagiarism
glossary	amateur	virus

Assessment	Formative Assessment: Sketch a Computer Keyboard
	     1. Students will be assessed by verbally answering questions about today's lesson.
	     2. Students will sketch a computer keyboard onto drawing paper.

Additional Information	**Accommodations and Modifications** The librarian will assist students as needed. Students in need of extra help will receive interventions consisting of varied instructional strategies. **Strategy of the Week:** Provide notes on computer skills and Internet resources for at-home use. **Early Finishers** Students will practice the academic vocabulary words listed above.

Worksheet 4G

"Internet Resources and Computer Skills- Part 3 (Keyboard Practice)"

DIRECTIONS:

Write the numbers and alphabet in the grey area of the computer keyboard below. As a bonus activity, fill in the rest of the keyboard and/or change the keyboard to match the computer keyboards at your school (keyboards may vary).

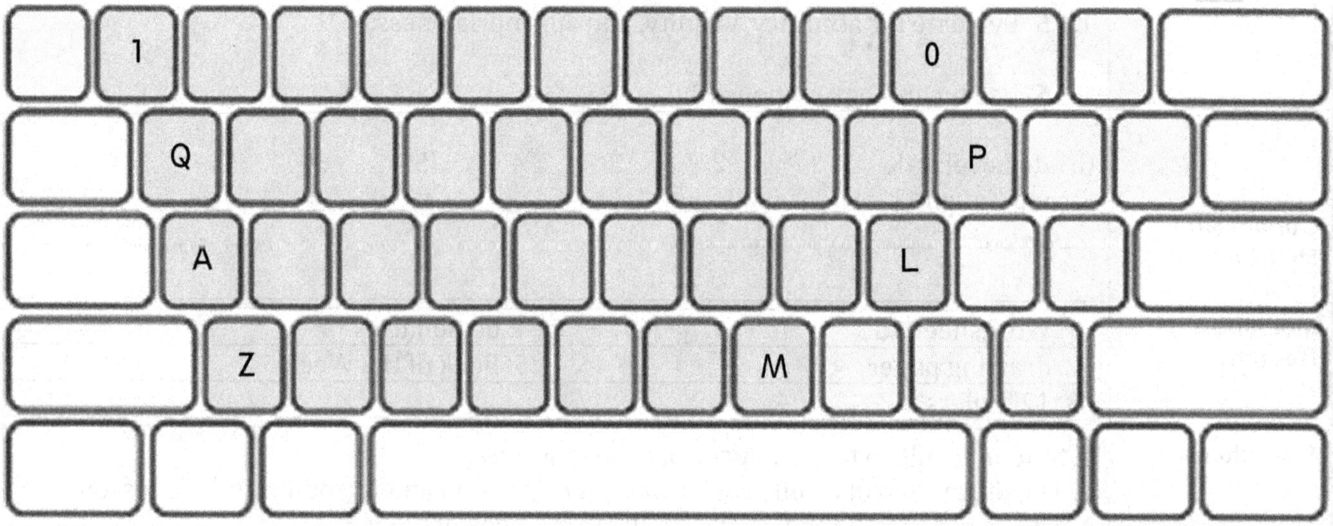

Vocabulary

remark	network	microfilm
primary	submissive	plagiarism
glossary	amateur	virus

Week 4H

Grade Level: K-6th **Subject: Library Skills** **Teacher/Librarian:**

MONDAY- FRIDAY
Title: "Newbery, Caldecott, and Other Literary Awards"

Objective

"I can" statement

Students will be able to compare and contrast the Newbery, Caldecott, and other literary awards.

I can describe the Newbery, Caldecott, and other literary awards.

LIBRARY Standards

4.1.3 Respond in various formats and genres.

4.1.7 Use social networks and information tools.

Current State Standards

Grade Level: K 1st 2nd 3rd 4th 5th 6th
Strand Taught: [ ] ______________________________
____

Materials Needed

1. Worksheet 4H	4. Newbery Award-Winning Books
2. sticky notes	5. Book of the Week:
3. Caldecott Award-Winning Books	

Procedures

1. Students will go to the appropriate seating area.
2. The librarian will briefly review last week's lesson and introduce today's lesson.
3. The librarian will read an excerpt from the book of the week.
4. Students will verbally answer questions about the book.
5. Students will use Worksheet 4H to learn about this week's objective.
6. If time permits, students will practice their vocabulary words.
7. Students will turn in all library books for the year .

Assignment

Complete Worksheet 4H and review the vocabulary words.

Vocabulary Words

search	privilege	benevolent
award	checkout	media
recall	summary	spontaneity

Assessment

Formative Assessment: Compare and Contrast Bubbles

1. As a group, students will draw cartoon characters with speech bubbles on sticky notes to compare and contrast the Newbery and Caldecott awards.

Additional Information

Accommodations and Modifications
The librarian will assist students as needed. Students in need of extra help will receive interventions consisting of varied instructional strategies.
Strategy of the Week:
Provide additional graphic organizers and writing space for writing about the awards.
Early Finishers
Students will practice the academic vocabulary words listed above.

Worksheet 4H

"Newbery, Caldecott, and Other Literary Awards"

DIRECTIONS:

Inside the circles, compare and contrast the Newbery Award and the Caldecott Award.

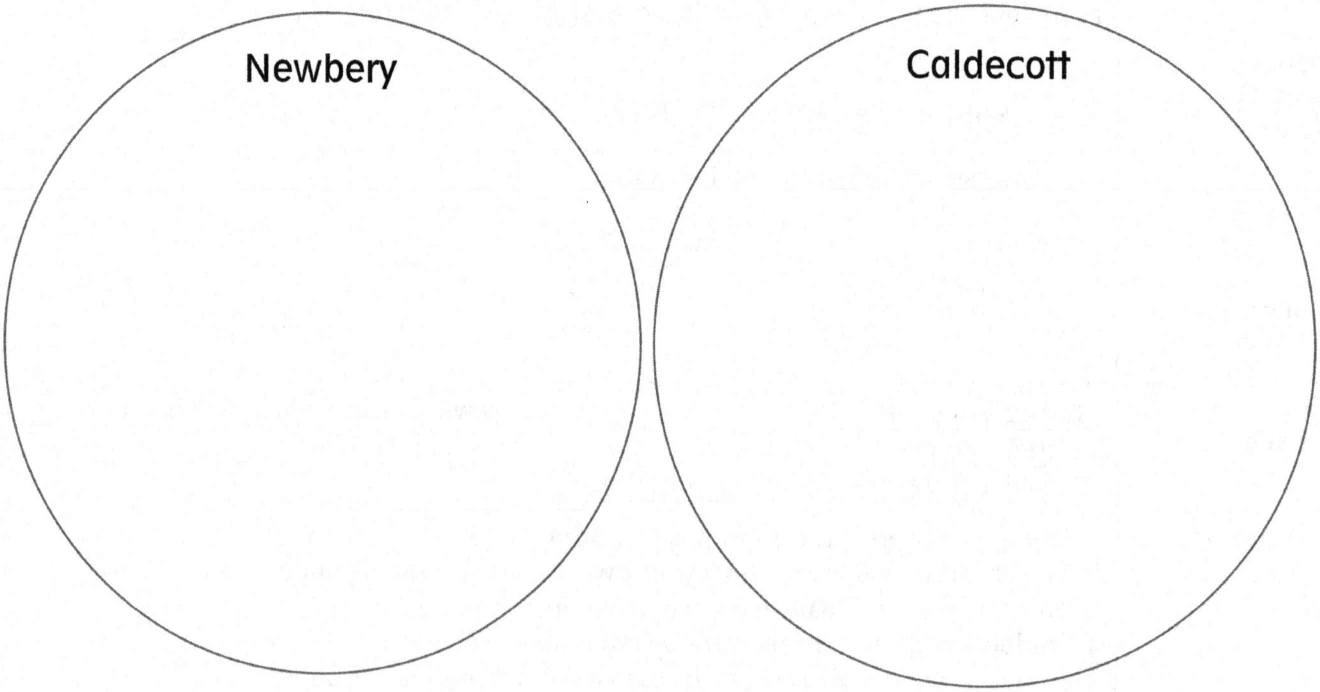

Vocabulary

search	privilege	benevolent
award	checkout	media
recall	summary	spontaneity

Grade Level: K-6th   **Subject: Library Skills**   **Teacher/Librarian:**

<table>
<tr>
<td colspan="2" align="center">MONDAY- FRIDAY
Title: "Mini-Book Report 2"</td>
</tr>
<tr>
<td>Objective

"I can" statement</td>
<td>Students will be able to write one mini-book report about a biography.

I can write one mini-book report about a biography.</td>
</tr>
<tr>
<td>LIBRARY Standards

Current State Standards</td>
<td>3.1.1 Reflect on the learning.

4.1.8 Use formats to express learning

Grade Level: K   1st   2nd   3rd   4th   5th   6th
Strand Taught: [   ] _____

_____</td>
</tr>
<tr>
<td>Materials Needed</td>
<td>
<table>
<tr><td>1. Worksheet 4I</td><td>4. dictionaries</td></tr>
<tr><td>2. notebook paper</td><td>5. Book of the Week:</td></tr>
<tr><td>3. biographies</td><td></td></tr>
</table>
</td>
</tr>
<tr>
<td>Procedures</td>
<td>1. Students will go to the appropriate seating area.
2. The librarian will briefly review last week's lesson and introduce today's lesson.
3. The librarian will read an excerpt from the book of the week.
4. Students will verbally answer questions about the book.
5. Students will use Worksheet 4I to learn about this week's objective.
6. If time permits, students will practice vocabulary words.
7. Students will turn in all library books for the year.</td>
</tr>
<tr>
<td>Assignment</td>
<td>Complete Worksheet 4I and review the vocabulary words.

Vocabulary Words
<table>
<tr><td>imitate</td><td>disdain</td><td>circulation</td></tr>
<tr><td>overdue</td><td>formulate</td><td>obstacle</td></tr>
<tr><td>signal</td><td>exaggeration</td><td>restrained</td></tr>
</table>
</td>
</tr>
<tr>
<td>Assessment</td>
<td>Formative Assessment: Name 5 Things- End of the Year Summary
    1. Students will be assessed by verbally answering questions about the book.
    2. As a group, students will name 5 things they learned in library class this year.</td>
</tr>
<tr>
<td>Additional Information</td>
<td align="center">Accommodations and Modifications
The librarian will assist students as needed. Students in need of extra help will receive interventions consisting of varied instructional strategies.
Strategy of the Week:
Provide additional graphic organizers and writing space.
Early Finishers
Students will practice the academic vocabulary words listed above.</td>
</tr>
</table>

Worksheet 4I

"Mini-Book Report 2"

Non-fiction Book

Book Title: ____________________ Author: ______________ No. of Pages: __________

Write five facts you learned from this book.

1.

2.

3.

4.

5.

Write two vocabulary words from the book. Include the word's definition.

1.

2.

Evaluate the book : 1 2 3 4 5 6 7 8 9 10

Vocabulary

imitate	disdain	circulation
overdue	formulate	obstacle
signal	exaggeration	restrained

Appendix A- Yearly Curriculum Map

1st 9 Weeks	**1A. ✓Welcome to the Library** **✓Library Rules** **1B. ✓Book Care Basics** **✓Library Rules Review** **1C. ✓Library Helpers:** **✓Shelf Markers, Book Ends, and Library Cards** **1D. ✓Fiction** **✓Non-fiction** **1E. ✓Library Catalog Searches** **1F. ✓Internet Resources** **✓Computer Skills** **1G. ✓Story Elements** **1H. ✓The Dewey Decimal Classification System** **1I. ✓Reference Books**
2nd 9 Weeks	**2A. ✓Intellectual Property** **✓Copyright Info** **2B. ✓Maps, Globes, and Atlases- Part 1** **2C. ✓Magazines** **2D. ✓Story Predictions** **2E. ✓Mystery Books** **2F. ✓Internet Resources** **✓Computer Skills-Part 2** **2G. ✓Table of Contents** **✓Index** **2H. ✓Poems and Poetry** **2I. ✓Mini- Book Report 1 (Fiction Book Report)**

3rd 9 Weeks	**3A. ✓Library Vocabulary** **✓Blurbs** **3B. ✓Dewey Decimal Classification System-Part 2** **3C. ✓Fairy Tales & Folk Tales** **3D. ✓Biographies** **3E. ✓Newspaper Articles** **✓Parts of a Newspaper** **3F. ✓Graphic Novels** **✓Comic Books** **3G. ✓Dictionary** **✓Thesaurus** **3H. ✓Maps, Globes, and Atlases- Part 2** **3I. ✓Using an Encyclopedia**
4th 9 Weeks	**4A. ✓Library Safety** **✓Library Rules Review** **4B. ✓Copyright Review** **✓Intellectual Property** **✓Ethics in the Library** **4C. ✓Author Study- Dr. Seuss** **4D. ✓Mini-Books-Part 1** **✓Front cover, back cover, and spine** **4E. ✓Mini-Books-Part 2** **✓Interior Pages** **4F. ✓Book Fair** **✓Reading Fair Practice** **4G. ✓Internet Resources** **✓Computer Skills- Part 3** **✓Keyboard Practice** **4H. ✓Newbery Award** **✓Caldecott Award** **✓Other Literary Awards** **4I. ✓Mini-Book Report 2** **✓Non-fiction Book Report**

Appendix B- Circulation Desk Poster Pad Format

(green) **(red)**

These new circulation desk poster pads were designed to make book check in and check out easier. When students approach the circulation desk, they can either put their book(s) and library card on the green check out pad or put their book(s) on the red check in pad. On the green check out pad, there is a space for students to place their library cards. With the Dr. Gaines circulation desk pads, book checkout can take as little as 2 seconds!

*** Dr. Gaines's Circulation Desk Poster Pads will be available for sale worldwide in the fall of 2019.**

Appendix C- Library Card Template #1

Elementary School LIBRARY CARD

Name: _____

Grade: K 1st 2nd 3rd 4th 5th 6th
☐ ☐ ☐ ☐ ☐ ☐ ☐

Goal: _____

Barcode

(add barcode here)

K
◎

| 1.0 | 1.1 | 1.2 | 1.3 | 1.4 | 1.5 | 1.6 | 1.7 | 1.8 | 1.9 |
| ◎ | ◎ | ◎ | ◎ | ◎ | ◎ | ◎ | ◎ | ◎ | ◎ |

| 2.0 | 2.1 | 2.2 | 2.3 | 2.4 | 2.5 | 2.6 | 2.7 | 2.8 | 2.9 |
| ◎ | ◎ | ◎ | ◎ | ◎ | ◎ | ◎ | ◎ | ◎ | ◎ |

| 3.0 | 3.1 | 3.2 | 3.3 | 3.4 | 3.5 | 3.6 | 3.7 | 3.8 | 3.9 |
| ◎ | ◎ | ◎ | ◎ | ◎ | ◎ | ◎ | ◎ | ◎ | ◎ |

| 4.0 | 4.1 | 4.2 | 4.3 | 4.4 | 4.5 | 4.6 | 4.7 | 4.8 | 4.9 |
| ◎ | ◎ | ◎ | ◎ | ◎ | ◎ | ◎ | ◎ | ◎ | ◎ |

| 5.0 | 5.1 | 5.2 | 5.3 | 5.4 | 5.5 | 5.6 | 5.7 | 5.8 | 5.9 |
| ◎ | ◎ | ◎ | ◎ | ◎ | ◎ | ◎ | ◎ | ◎ | ◎ |

| 6.0 | 6.1 | 6.2 | 6.3 | 6.4 | 6.5 | 6.6 | 6.7 | 6.8 | 6.9 |
| ◎ | ◎ | ◎ | ◎ | ◎ | ◎ | ◎ | ◎ | ◎ | ◎ |

7.0+
◎

*For best results, copy this template on cardstock for each student. Color-code the student's current ZPD (reading levels) onto the card using different colored markers. Print out, cut out, and attach each student's barcode to the barcode area using clear tape. NOTE: Some book scanners will have difficulty scanning barcodes if the barcode is laminated onto the library card.

Appendix D- Library Card Template #2

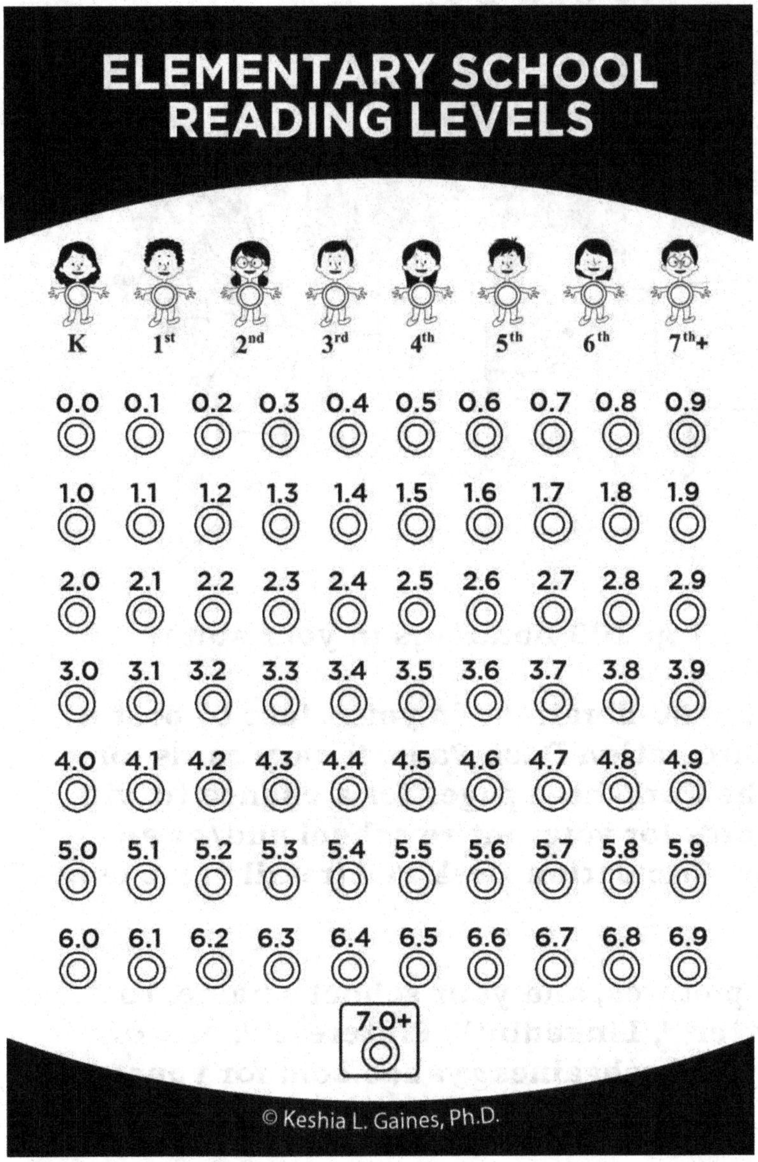

***For best results, copy this template on cardstock for each student. Color-code the student's current ZPD (reading levels) onto the card using different colored markers. Print out, cut out, and attach each student's barcode to the barcode area using clear tape. NOTE: Some book scanners will have difficulty scanning barcodes if the barcode is laminated onto the library card.**

Appendix E- Top 100 Librarian Challenge

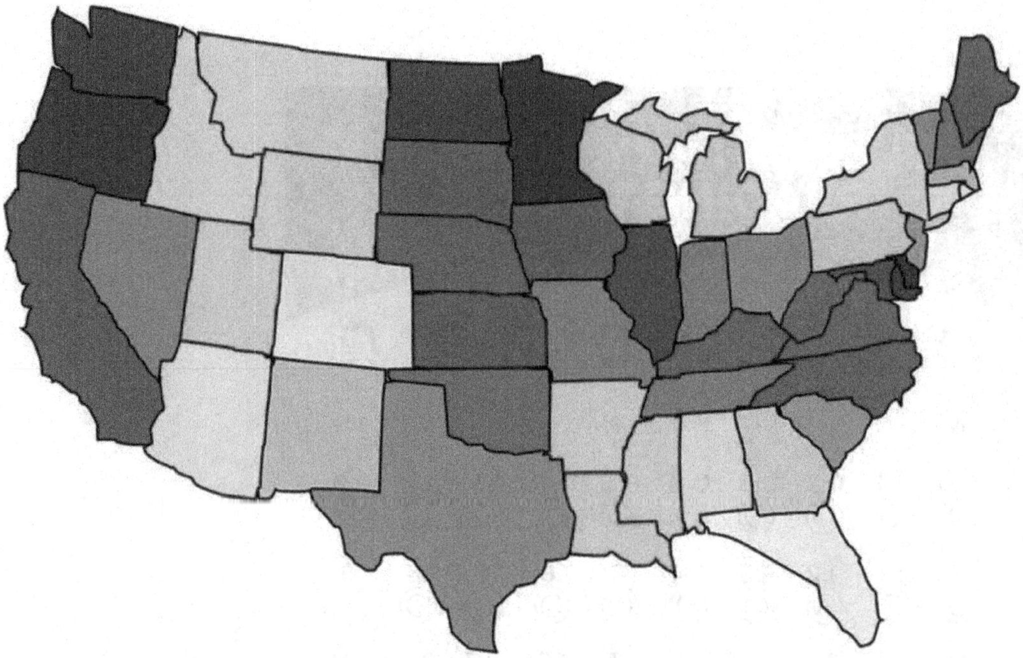

Are you one of the Top 100 librarians in your state?

Be one of the first 100 librarians in your state to post a picture of your Circulation Desk Pads, library cards, or students using the worksheet pages for a chance to win custom library cards for your entire school and/or an official Dr. Gaines Circulation Desk Pad (retail value over $310.00)!

Post your name, pictures, and your school's name, to Facebook™, Twitter™, LinkedIn™, Pinterest™, etc. or e-mail your entry to keshgaines@yahoo.com for your chance to win!

#Top100Librarian

Buy a copy of Dr. Gaines's other books:

Why are Students Not Learning on the School Bus?

Learning on the School Bus

www.iuniverse.com

www.amazon.com

www.barnesandnoble.com

WAIT!

Order a copy of The Dr. Keshia Gaines Magazine!

Enjoy helpful tips and positive inspiration from celebrity author Dr. Keshia Gaines. This quarterly mini-magazine is every busy reader's go-to-guide for health & nutrition, money-saving tips, fun craft projects, entertainment, and more! Also, this super-short magazine features Dr. Gaines's famous word search puzzle in every issue!

www.magcloud.com
www.facebook.com/drgainesmagazine

Printed in the United States
By Bookmasters